... Experiencing Greater Realities

Giving Change a Chance

... Experiencing Greater Realities

Giving Change a Chance

Abolade Abby Adeyemi

GIVING CHANGE A CHANCE
...Experiencing Greater Realities

Copyright © Abolade Abby Adeyemi, 2024

All rights reserved. No part of this publication may be reproduced, stored in a retrieval system, or transmitted in any form or by any means, electronic, mechanical, photocopying, recording, or otherwise, without written permission of the author and publisher.

Names, characters, businesses, places, events, locales, and incidents are either the products of the author's imagination or used in a fictitious manner. Any resemblance to actual persons, living or dead, or actual events is purely coincidental.

Published by Abolade Abby Adeyemi, Edmonton, Canada

abbyadeyemi.com

ISBN:
    Paperback   978-1-77354-597-4
        ebook   978-1-77354-598-1

Publication assistance by

PageMaster.ca

Dedication

I dedicate this book to God, the Author and Finisher of our faith. Your grace and guidance have been the foundation upon which this work stands. Your unchanging love and unwavering support have been my source of strength and inspiration.

To the One who makes all things new, thank you for teaching me to embrace change with courage and faith. May this book serve as a testament to Your transformative power and a beacon of hope for all who seek renewal and growth.

In Your name, I offer this work as an act worship and a reflection of your boundless mercy.

To God be the glory

Contents

Acknowledgment 1

First Words 3

INTRODUCTION
Discover the Power of Embracing Change 4

SECTION ONE:
Change is Neither Bad nor Good 6

CHAPTER 1
What is Change? 7

CHAPTER 2
Why Are We Afraid of it? 21

CHAPTER 3
What Happens if we Run from Change? 31

SECTION TWO
Common Changes We Face 40

CHAPTER 4
Financial Changes 41

CHAPTER 5
Career/Business Changes 48

CHAPTER 6
Health Challenges 52

CHAPTER 7
Relationships Changes 61

CHAPTER 8
Family Changes 65

CHAPTER 9
Spirituality Changes 71

Section Three
Embracing Change..77

Chapter 10
Giving Change a Chance..79

Chapter 11
Being Strong – Resilience 84

Chapter 12
Step 1 – Recognize the Change 91

Chapter 13
Step 2 – Define The Change..99

Chapter 14
Step 3 – Don't Let the Change Define You 106

Chapter 15
Step 4 – Weigh The Pros And Cons Of Taking Action...................111

Chapter 16
Step 5 – Make The Proper Preparations...115

Chapter 17
Step 6 – Take Action 119

Chapter 18
Step 7 – Practice Proper Maintenance 128

Conclusion 136
Final Words 138
About the Book 140
About the Author 141

Acknowledgment

With immense gratitude and heartfelt appreciation, I extend my deepest thanks to all who have played a role in the creation and realization of my debut book. To my cherished family, especially my four beautiful children; your unwavering support, love, and understanding have been my greatest inspiration and motivation throughout this journey. To my dear husband; your constant encouragement and belief in my abilities have been the bedrock upon which I've built my dreams.

I am indebted to my mentors, colleagues, and friends for their invaluable guidance, wisdom, and encouragement. As a mother and wife, balancing the demands of family life with the pursuit of academic and professional endeavors has been a challenge, but your unwavering support and understanding have made it all possible.

To the countless individuals within the healthcare and senior care communities; your tireless dedication to improving the lives of others has inspired me beyond measure. As a senior care advocate and public health mogul, I am humbled by the opportunity to contribute to the betterment of the society, and I am committed to continuing this important work.

Finally, to all those who have generously supported my philanthropic endeavors and shared in my enthusiasm for making a positive impact in the world, I am profoundly grateful. Your belief in me and my vision have fueled my passion and determination to effect meaningful changes.

With deepest appreciation for your unwavering support, love, and encouragement, I hereby dedicate this book to each and everyone of you.

Abolade Adeyemi
MD/Ph.D. Holder
Senior Care Advocate
Public Health Consultant

First Words

I've seen people struggle with accepting changes in their lives. I've seen them spend days feeling sad and upset about things that aren't worth feeling that way for. Many times, challenges in life lead to exciting new places if you handle them well. That's why I decided to write this book – to help as many people as possible come out of sadness and depression.

Change isn't always good or bad. It's actually a blank page waiting for your thoughts to fill it. It can make you feel down or lift you up, depending on how you see it. As you read this book, get ready for a big change on how you think. Open your heart and mind to learn, and get ready to feel happier and fulfilled. I want you to know that I'm writing this with the hope of making you really happy, helping you face challenges, and enjoying the victories that come with change.

So, as you read this book and learn about change, know that you're taking a step towards a better life. Change won't be something scary anymore – it'll be like a friend helping you on your journey.

From,
Abolade Adeyemi

INTRODUCTION

Discover the Power of Embracing Change

Are you standing on the crossroads of change – wondering if it's happening to you or if you're the one causing it? Are you facing change head-on, or are you running from it? Life is a continuous shifting landscape, where change is an unyielding force. It can bring joy or sorrow, laughter or tears, fear or confidence and so much more.

You see, life is a stage, and change is the spotlight that turns on at unexpected moments. How you react to it becomes your performance, your chance to shine or shrink away. Have you heard of Heraclitus, a wise philosopher from ancient Greece? He lived in the city of Ephesus over two thousand years ago. His words might have faded, but his message endures: "Change is constant. Nothing remains the same."

Whether it's a small shift or a monumental transformation, the key lies in your reaction. Will you choose optimism or pessimism, hope or despair, fear or faith, cowardice or courage? Will you allow fear to cripple you, or will you step into the unknown with courage and determination?

Welcome to the world of "Giving Change a Chance." In these pages, you will uncover the secrets of mastering change. You see, the truth is that change isn't just an external force – it's an opportunity for you to rise. It's an opportunity to paint your resilience, your growth, and your triumph. This book is your guide through the tumultuous sea of Change. It doesn't matter what storm you have faced or what challenges you have encountered. What matters is how you navigate them. And let me assure you, by embracing the principles within these pages, victory is not a distant dream – it's a reality waiting for you.

With carefully written insights, practical strategies, and real-life examples, this book brings to you the great effect of embracing change. We have all had our share of setbacks, but this is your chance to rise above them. Each chapter is a step towards harnessing the power of change for your benefit. No matter what you have been through, I want you to know that by embracing the principles shared in this book, you will triumph over adversity. I don't say this lightly, but with conviction – you will emerge victorious.

So, as you embark on this journey of transformation, remember that change whether good or bad is not your enemy – it is your ally. And with the right mindset and tools, you will not only face change but use it to your advantage. Get ready to unleash the power within you, to embrace the unpredictable, and to emerge as a victor in the ever-changing battles of life.

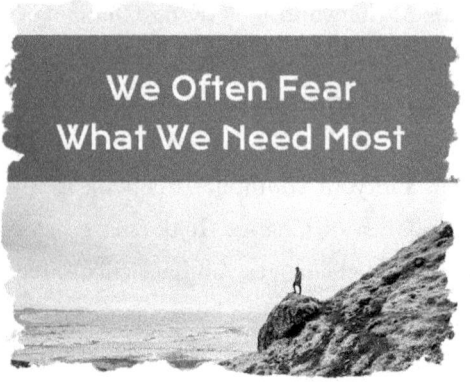

We Often Fear What We Need Most

SECTION ONE:

Change is Neither Bad nor Good

When we say "change is neither bad nor good," we mean that change itself doesn't come with a label of being only good or only bad. It's more about how you think about it and how it affects your feelings. Just like the crayons, it's about how you use them to make something wonderful. Sometimes change challenges us, but it can also bring positive things if we look at it in a certain way.

Chapter 1

What is Change?

"Change is not inherently negative or positive; it's simply a shift from what was to what will be."

I have come to realize that the mere mention of the word "change" has a way of creating a curious and anxious effect on many of us. It's as if it makes us tremble with fear, and before we know it our minds race back to all those moments when change seemed to have conspired against us and crated negative scenarios. The memory of the uncertainty, the struggles, and the unfamiliar territory fills us with a sense of trepidation. It's almost as if our minds have been trained to associate change with difficulty and discomfort. But here's the thing – that's not the only way to see it, and it's time we embraced a different perspective.

But sincerely speaking change is just a normal, natural and foundational part of life, you really do not have to fear it, in fact let's see a dictionary definition of change rhythm.

The Trusted Oxford language dictionary defines change as this:

- Verb – Make different; alter or modify. Replace something with something else; substitute one thing for another.
- Noun – The act or instance of making or becoming different.

Did you notice the definition does not see change as being negative or positive? It's simply something different from what already existed.

What am I trying to say? Okay look at it this way, you can change your wardrobe; If you discover you have type II diabetes, you will probably need to change your diet and add an exercise to your routine.

If you don't like the fees, you can change what bank you do business with.

I believe you now get my point, the definition of change doesn't say it has to be positive or negative. It just has to be an alternate reality to what you were used to experiencing.

So why have you always been scared of the word, take another look at those definitions, do they talk about emotional upheaval? Is there anywhere in those definitions that declares your life is over if the change is terrible? Does the Oxford Dictionary mention that positive change is easier to accept than its negative counterpart? Of course not!

What's that? You don't believe it? Tell that to the lottery winners who believed that millions of dollars would positively transform their lives. Many of them claimed that winning the lottery was the worst thing that ever happened to them. Many of them found that what looked like a beautiful miracle was the "gift" that ruined their relationships, families, and lives.

You see, the major reason people fear change is because they are not the ones orchestrating and causing the change, if you are the one causing the change, then there is no need to fear or be anxious because you are actually in control – and being in control is a good thing. I mean, wouldn't you rather be the one making your desired change than wait for fate to turn and twist you in any direction it wants?

If change is constant and inevitable, and it definitely is, why not make your own changes? Embrace the idea of controlling how your life changes rather than sitting back and waiting for some negative change you have to deal with.

You see, seasons change, days turn into nights, and time marches forward. I tell you the truth change is a constant, it is a continuous melody that proves to us that life is happening and we are not dead, as long as the earth remain, change will always happen, you are growing, you are going to school, your knowledge is changing, you will soon get married and then have kids, your life is changing.

Types of Change

Reversible Change – This is a change that is not permanent

Let's talk about something really important – reversible change. You know, those situations that can knock you off balance and make you feel like everything's falling apart. But guess what? You have got more power than you might think. Reversible change is all about those shifts that might hit hard at first, but the cool part is that you have the ability to turn them around.

Reversible changes many times might just come out of nowhere; losing your job, for example, can feel like a huge setback. It's natural to feel down about it, but the thing is, you are not stuck there forever. Yes, it's tough, and it's okay to feel upset. However, the key point here is that you can take action to improve the situation. You can learn new skills, market yourself differently, and find another job. Reversible change means that even though it might feel like your world is crashing down, you have the tools to rebuild it.

Now, let's talk money. Losing money is many times really frustrating, and you might feel as though things will never get better. But remember, you are not defined by your losses. You are defined by how you bounce back from them. Reversible change means that even though you are facing setbacks, you have the chance to recover and move forward.

Think of reversible change as a passing storm. Yes, it might make you uncomfortable and unsure, but it's not a never-ending downpour. You have the ability to shield yourself from the storm and find ways to get back on track. Reversible change is all about realizing that you are not at the mercy of circumstances. You have the ability to take control and make things better.

In a nutshell, reversible change is a challenge that comes with an opportunity to grow. It's a test of your resilience and determination, it's a change you can do something about. It might feel comparable to facing huge obstacles, but remember that you have the power and ability to overcome them. Reversible change means that even though life might throw you off course, you can steer yourself back in the right direction. So, next time you encounter a reversible change, remember that you are not helpless. You are capable of taking charge, making decisions, and turning things around. It's all about realizing that even though a change is tough, it's not the end of the road. You are equipped with the power to change the course of your life and transform challenges into stepping stones towards a brighter future.

Reversible changes are never hopeless

A story is told that in the vibrant city of Calabar, Nigeria, during the year 2000, lived a couple named John and Ada. They were deeply in love, and their days were filled with laughter, dreams, and the promise of a bright future ahead.

However, their story took an unexpected turn when Ada fell ill. It wasn't just a simple sickness; it was cancer, a word that cast a heavy shadow over their lives. John, a loving and caring husband, was shattered by the news. The thought of seeing his beloved Ada suffer and wither away was a blow that struck his heart like a hammer. As the days went by, John found himself torn between his love for Ada and his inability to watch her endure the pain that cancer brought. He believed that leaving her might spare them both from the agony of witnessing her decline. His heart ached at the thought of letting her go, but he thought it might be the only way to protect himself from the impending heartbreak.

Six months passed, marked by a cloud of uncertainty that hovered over their home. One day, a friend named Michael came to visit John. They shared stories, laughs, and a few drinks. As the evening wore on, Michael leaned in and whispered something that would change John's perspective forever.

"John," Michael said gently, "there's a glimmer of hope for Ada, my friend. If you can get her to a certain city, there might be a chance to turn things around." John's heart raced as he absorbed Michael's words. A glimmer of hope? A chance to change their fate?

It was like a spark of light in the darkness that had engulfed their lives. Suddenly, the weight on John's shoulders seemed a bit lighter. He realized that maybe, just maybe, their situation wasn't as hopeless as he had thought.

With renewed determination, John felt a surge of energy coursing through him. He was no longer trapped in the cage of despair. He now knew that there was something he could do, a step he could take to fight for Ada's life. His realization was a wakeup call – a reminder that he didn't have to remain in the depths of sorrow when there was a chance for change.

Without a moment's hesitation, John made up his mind. He was going to take action, to embark on a journey that would require faith, resilience, and unwavering persistence. He knew that it wouldn't be easy, but he was willing to do whatever it took to save Ada.

Days turned into weeks as John navigated the challenges of arranging the trip to the city of hope. It was a journey filled with uncertainties, doubts, and moments of fear. However, his love for Ada fueled his determination, and he pressed on with the unwavering belief that change was possible.

Finally, the day arrived when John and Ada set out on their journey. It was a journey not just of miles, but of hope and healing. With every step, John's heart beat with anticipation, praying that this path would lead them to the miracle they so desperately sought. Months went by, and the treatment in the city of hope proved to be a beacon of light in their darkest hour. Ada's health gradually improved, and the cloud of cancer began to lift. The journey that had begun with a dim light of hope now blossomed into a radiant sunrise of joy.

John's persistence, his refusal to give in to despair, had paid off. The couple emerged from the shadows of sickness into the warmth of renewed life. Their love story, once marred by the threat of loss, now stood as a testament to the power of change, action, and unwavering faith.

This tale of John and Ada teaches us that even in the face of the most challenging circumstances, we have the power to create change. Crying and worrying does not solve our problems, but taking action, fueled by love and hope will lead us to a better tomorrow. Just as John leaped into action when he discovered a glimmer of hope, we too can leap into the unknown with the belief that change is possible, and that joy can emerge from the darkest of times.

Irreversible Change – When some events happen, they stay that way, such are seen as irreversible changes. These are the changes that stick around no matter what you do. They are similar to marks left in wet cement – once they are there, they stay. It's important to understand these changes because they are a bit different from the ones we can fix.

Irreversible Changes are doors that are closed and locked behind you. If you lose your job, you will work hard to find another one. There's a chance to make things better, to find a new chance. But imagine losing your mom or dad. That's a whole different story. You can't just find another one. It's as if a page is torn from the book of your life, and you can't bring it back no matter how much you search.

Think about it as a favorite toy from when you were a kid. If you lose it, no matter how much you look, that exact toy is gone. Sure, you can find something similar, but the original one is gone for good. Irreversible changes are like that – they are a part of your life that can't be changed.

Losing someone close is like a piece of your heart going missing. It's like a puzzle with a piece that's been taken away, and that piece can never be found again. Yes, you might find new pieces to add, like friends and loved ones who support you, but the missing piece will always be missing, these kinds of changes are synonymous to a tattoo on your skin – permanent and not changeable. It's a fact of life that can be hard to accept.

Imagine a sunset. Once the sun goes down, you can't make it rise again at that moment. You have to wait for a new day. Irreversible Changes are like that sunset – they mark the end of something, the closing of a door that won't open again. But even in the weight of Irreversible Changes, there's a chance to find strength and be okay with it. It's about understanding that even if you can't change the past, you can choose how to react. It's like looking at a painting and focusing on the colors that still look nice, instead of the ones that have faded.

In short, irreversible changes are like a chapter that's written and closed. It's about realizing that life has limits, that there are moments we can't change. But within this understanding, there's a chance to grow – to value what you have, to remember the good times, and to find a way to keep going.

When you face irreversible changes, let yourself feel, process, and find your own way to feel better. Remember, life is a picture made with both changeable and unchangeable threads. Each thread, no matter how it is, makes your story beautiful. While you can't change the unchangeable, you can deal with it gracefully, remembering the past while moving forward with hope and strength.

Shadows of Irreversible Changes

You must learn to see life from the positive point of view, the reason I am reviewing these negative effects is so that you can know them and guide against them, running away doesn't change things so let's face reality and deal with it. I mean change can comes with some discomforts and terrors but with knowledge about this discomforts and terrors we can accurately deal with them and come out stronger than ever before. Some of these shadows of irreversible changes include.

Loss and Grief: Irreversible change often leads to profound loss, triggering a deep sense of grief. Whether it's the passing of a loved one or the end of a significant phase in life, the experience of loss can be all-encompassing. The reality that we can't reverse these changes can intensify our grief, making it difficult to come to terms with the new reality.

Inescapable Endings: Unlike reversible changes, irreversible ones mark the end of something that cannot be undone. This finality can be unsettling, as it signifies a closure that holds no possibility of reversal. The awareness that this chapter has concluded can generate feelings of sadness and apprehension about what lies ahead.

Unanswered Questions: The uncertainty surrounding irreversible change often gives rise to unanswered questions. We find ourselves pondering the "whys" and "hows" of the situation. These questions can fuel a sense of unease, as we grapple with the absence of clear explanations and struggle to make sense of the change.

Regret and What-ifs: The permanence of irreversible change evokes feelings of regret and a preoccupation with "what could have been." The inability to alter the course of events may lead us to second-guess our decisions and actions. This longing for alternate outcomes has the power to hinder our ability to accept the change as it is.

Permanence of Pain: Unlike reversible changes that can be rectified, the pain associated with irreversible change might persist. The anguish of loss or significant life alterations can remain a constant companion. This enduring pain also casts a shadow over our everyday experiences, making it challenging to find solace.

Sense of Powerlessness: Irreversible change also evokes a sense of powerlessness, leaving us feeling helpless in the face of circumstances we can't control. This lack of agency can foster frustration and exacerbate the emotional toll of the change. The absence of options to reverse the situation can intensify feelings of vulnerability.

Fear of the Unknown: The uncertainty that accompanies irreversible change can ignite a fear of the unknown. The inability to predict what lies ahead can be unsettling, as we venture into uncharted territory. This fear can amplify the emotional strain of the change, generating apprehension about the future.

Longing for Reversibility: The desire to undo irreversible change can become a persistent thought pattern. The yearning to turn back time and reverse the course of events can dominate our thoughts, making it difficult to accept the change as a part of our reality. This longing can hinder our ability to find closure.

Challenges in Acceptance: Coming to terms with irreversible change can be an arduous process. The acceptance of a new reality, one that cannot be undone, might require considerable emotional effort. The struggle to embrace the change as an integral part of our journey can impede our ability to heal and move forward.

Impact on Identity: Irreversible change can influence our sense of self and identity. Significant life alterations can reshape the way we perceive ourselves, leading to an identity crisis of sorts. The shifts in our circumstances can prompt introspection and a reevaluation of who we are in the face of these changes.

Amidst these challenges, it's essential to acknowledge that while irreversible change can bring difficulties, it also carries the potential for growth and resilience. Just as a tree stands firm during a storm, you possess an innate ability to weather the emotional storms brought about by irreversible change. Recognizing the negative features while also acknowledging the capacity for transformation will provide a balanced perspective.

As you go through this complexities of irreversible change, seeking support and adopting healthy coping strategies will make a significant difference and ensure that you emerge triumphant. Grief counseling, therapy, and connecting with individuals who have experienced similar changes has a remarkable way of offering solace and guidance. Additionally, focusing on personal growth, finding meaning in the experience, and cultivating resilience will empower you to face the unchangeable with courage and determination.

Yes you can't rewrite the past or reverse irreversible change, yet you have the capacity to shape your responses and attitudes towards it. Embracing these challenges as part of your unique journey will lead to a deeper understanding of yourself and your capacity to overcome these shadows. You see, just as a diamond is formed under pressure, your ability to thrive in the face of irreversible change has the power to illuminate your strength and resilience, reminding you that you are capable of transforming challenges into opportunities for growth and personal evolution.

The Positive Aspects of Irreversible Changes

Although irreversible change often carries a weight of challenges, it's essential to recognize that within its depths lie hidden strengths and positive aspects that can shape your personal growth and journey. Now let us see some of these positive features.

Resilience and Inner Strength: Irreversible change has a way of revealing our inner reservoirs of strength. When faced with circumstances we can't alter, we tap into our innate resilience, discovering our ability to endure and adapt. Just as a tree bends in the wind but remains rooted, we too find the strength to weather the storm.

Empathy and Compassion: Going through irreversible change equips us with a deeper understanding of others' struggles. This heightened empathy and compassion stem from our own experiences of loss and change. This newfound empathy enables us to connect with others on a profound level, offering support and understanding.

Reevaluation of Priorities: Life's unchangeable moments often prompt a reevaluation of our priorities. We begin to discern what truly matters and shed the trivial concerns. It's like cleaning out a cluttered room, making space for what holds genuine value. This shift in perspective leads to a more intentional and fulfilling life.

Enhanced Problem-Solving Skills: Navigating irreversible change encourages the development of robust problem-solving skills. When faced with unalterable circumstances, we're challenged to find creative solutions and alternative paths. This process hones our ability to think outside the box and adapt to new challenges.

Heightened Appreciation: Irreversible change fosters a heightened appreciation for life's fleeting moments. We learn to savor the present and cherish our relationships. Like capturing a

Change May Be Hard, But It Is Also Inevitable

fleeting sunset, we grasp the beauty of each passing day, aware of the impermanence that underscores our existence.

Transformation and Growth: Just as a caterpillar transforms into a butterfly, irreversible change has the potential to ignite profound personal growth. The challenges we face push us beyond our comfort zones, compelling us to embrace change and emerge stronger, wiser, and more resilient.

Discovery of Inner Reservoirs: When confronted with the unchangeable, we unearth untapped resources within ourselves. These resources may include courage, tenacity, and a renewed sense of purpose. It's like discovering a hidden treasure chest within us, brimming with the tools needed to navigate life's challenges.

Cultivation of Gratitude: Irreversible change often births a deep sense of gratitude. As we witness the impermanence of life, we become grateful for the moments we've had and the relationships we've cherished. This gratitude serves as a beacon of light amidst the darkness of change.

Fostering of Connections: The process of navigating irreversible change can lead to the formation of meaningful connections. We connect with those who have undergone similar experiences, finding solace and camaraderie in shared stories. These connections provide a support network that strengthens our resilience.

Deepened Spiritual Insight: Life's unchangeable moments often prompt introspection and spiritual exploration. We seek answers to profound questions about existence and purpose. This journey of self-discovery can lead to a deeper connection with our spiritual beliefs and a newfound sense of inner peace.

You are reminded that even amidst the challenges of life there is an opportunity for growth, connection, and transformation by embracing these positive aspects of irreversible change and also by focusing on these positive features, you can navigate life's unchangeable moments with a sense of hope, gratitude, and a steadfast faith in our capacity to thrive amidst adversity.

Chapter 2

Why Are We Afraid of it?

"Even in the face of positive change, our fear stems from the uncertainty it brings, the unknown territory that challenges our comfort zone."

There are a lot of reasons we fear change. You probably have your own motivating factors for resisting unpredictable and unforeseen change. Instead of looking at why we resist negative change, let's take a more positive situation.

We'll use a variation on an example from earlier.

Your boss calls you into her office. She says she's happy to inform you that you are being offered a wonderful promotion. It has more money and better benefits, and you will be doing less mind-numbing and physically grueling work than you did before.

You hadn't been expecting this. The news is fantastic and unexpected. Your boss says you will start in this great new position with a week's paid training. The company will foot the bill to fly you to a beautiful beachside resort. You will meet with others from the company who have been likewise promoted.

After a short daily class at a nearby training center, you can spend the rest of the day however you like. The company includes a per diem, so you have some money at your disposal.

This looks like a dream come true, but you hesitate. As your boss approaches with a smile to shake your hand, assuming you are going to take the position, you inform her that you need to think about it. She gets a look on her face as though she just sucked on a lemon. She can't imagine why someone in your position wouldn't immediately and enthusiastically accept the promotion. You ask her if you can take some time to think about it. She says that's fine, and you return to your familiar workstation.

What Happened?

Why aren't you greeting the situation positively? Most people would beg for this opportunity. Here you are looking at it as though there might be something not so positive in the offer. That's because you know the position means changing the hours you work. You will not be able to spend as much time with your children because of your shift change. That's not something you want to think about.

Your current coworkers are awesome. You guys get along so very well. Everyone watches each other's back, and going to work every day is an absolute joy. Who knows what the work environment will be like with your new coworkers?

What if you don't live up to expectations? You might get knocked back to your current position. Worse yet, your new job will have you making choices that could be potentially harmful to the company if you mess up. Could this new promotion end up getting you fired if you make a big mistake? Sometimes we're scared of change even when it seems wonderfully positive. Why?

Here are some of the most common reasons that people fear change.

It Makes You Nervous

It's completely natural to feel nervous about change, change represents movement into the unknown, which provokes anxiety and worry. When things are stable, we feel in control and know what to expect. But change disrupts this predictability and certainty. Most of us crave a predictable routine that allows us to plan and feel in command of our lives. Change turns everything upside down, inducing stress from losing our sense of stability - we start to worry that change will lead to outcomes we are unprepared for. It feels nerve-wracking to give up the assurance of the status quo, even when it is flawed.

Additionally, nerves arise from realizing change may reveal our flaws and weaknesses, exposes us to judgment and criticism if we fail to adapt smoothly. Since change brings the risk of failure, we get nervous about potential embarrassment or consequences to our reputation or self-image and such worry has the power to cripple actions.

Nerves also emerge as we wrestle against inertia, there is a strong temptation to cling to the familiar status quo rather than pushing beyond resistance. Breaking from stagnation requires fighting stubborn instincts. This internal conflict is nerve-wracking. Self-doubt fuels nervousness about whether we can actually implement planned changes.

Uncertainty

A major reason many fear change is the uncertainty it brings. When life is stable and predictable, we feel in control. But change means trading the known for the unknown. Instead of feeling confident about what to expect, we feel lost navigating uncharted waters. Venturing into the unfamiliar makes most people apprehensive. Our minds naturally focus on "What if?" imagining worst case scenarios. We worry about how change will impact every aspect of our lives. Without knowing what lies ahead, our anxiety amplifies the potential risks and downsides. This anticipatory stress serves an evolutionary purpose - uncertainty signaled danger to our ancestors. But today it hinders us from seizing opportunities for growth. We become so unsettled by vagueness and doubt that we prefer to remain in the safety of familiarity. Yet the certainty we cling to is an illusion. In reality, the only constant in life is change. By facing the unknown with courage, we can discover possibilities that fear would conceal.

Fear of Failure

Closely tied to the uncertainty of change is a fear of failure. When we step outside our comfort zones into new endeavors, there is no guarantee of success. Our efforts could lead nowhere, or even make things worse. And so we are hesitant to try, paralyzed by the risk of disappointment, wasted effort, or embarrassment. Behind this lies deeper fears - fear of judgment, of revealing our inadequacies, of losing status and respect. Fear of confirming the belief that we lack what it takes to adapt and succeed. Such failure would injure our pride and shake our self-confidence. In fact, even the fear of these consequences is enough to make us rigidly cling to the status quo. But the most successful people fail far more often than the rest. They recognize failure as a teacher, not a sentence. Each setback contains lessons to help them grow. By refusing failure its power to devastate us, we gain the courage to fail forward.

Fear of Success

Oddly, we may also fear the success that change could bring. Breaking out of old ruts means leaving behind an identity that, although unsatisfying, feels familiar. Success brings the unknown of a new self-image and set of expectations. We fear being unable to live up to that vision, of buckling under the pressure to achieve more than ever before. Or that others will grow jealous and undermine our success. Some worry they don't deserve success, or that achieving their goals means life will lose meaning. The risk of these unwanted consequences keeps many clinging to mediocrity. But if we ignore fear's false warnings, we can appreciate success without letting it change who we are. We can channel it into humility, gratitude and service.

Fear of Not Surviving Change

In ancient times, venturing into unfamiliar terrain could mean mortal danger. So our brains evolved a powerful risk-aversion to change. Though physically safer today, change still activates old primal fears of inadequate resources and tribal abandonment. We irrationally fear that the disruption of change will threaten our survival - that it will somehow leave us destitute and unable to provide for ourselves. At the same time, we fear exclusion by the group if we change, that we will lose the social ties that sustain us. This isolation would have been extremely hazardous for our ancestors, so we instinctively resist actions that could incur social disapproval or rejection. In reality, few changes today carry such extreme consequences. As we override those knee-jerk fears, we gain the adaptability that is now essential to survival in a world of constant change.

Fear of What Change Requires

Beyond just fearing the uncertainty of change, many also fear leaving behind the known and comfortable. Even when we want the end result, getting there means transitioning through an awkward and draining in-between stage. We must endure growing pains to form new habits and ways of thinking. Old behaviors and mindsets have to be dismantled before the new can solidify. This messy process feels threatening, even when the outcome is positive. We are tempted to avoid it through the instinct to favor what's familiar. But escaping stagnation necessitates pushing past that initial discomfort. With discipline and commitment, the discomfort of change soon transforms into a new, better routine. Progress requires accepting short-term difficulty for long-term gain.

Additionally, change forces us to give up comforting old pleasures and conveniences, and these are many times a great loss to us. We don't want to sacrifice things that make life easy and enjoyable, even when they hold us back. Letting go is painful, even when we have something better ahead. This is the fear of loss aversion - we prefer avoiding a small loss over realizing a larger gain. Accepting loss as a natural part of progress takes maturity and courage.

Change also demands heightened mental effort. Adapting to new situations strains our cognitive resources. Learning new skills and behaviors taxes our energies. Even positive change is draining in the short term. Our natural instinct is to conserve our limited time and energy where we can. Sticking to the familiar status quo feels easier. But resisting this urge for comfort is crucial for stepping out of stagnation. Muscles have to be pushed to grow stronger. The mind is no different. With discipline, the hard work required by change pays compounding dividends.

Beyond the internal challenges, other people may discourage change and growth. Wanting to preserve the status quo, they imply we are foolish for trying something new or outside convention. Their skepticism and disapproval only amplify our self-doubt. This social pressure provides justification to remain stagnant. However, allowing others to dictate our growth cedes control of our lives. The rewards of change remain obscured unless we retain the courage of conviction.

In summary, fearing change is human. But we should not let fear force us to languish. With awareness, we can honor our fears without surrendering to them. We can find the courage to progress through uncertainty into growth. For on the other side of discomfort awaits discovery, meaning, and fulfillment.

Finding Joy amidst Challenging Changes

There is no need to fear change all because it might come with some pains or unwanted circumstances, in this world that we live in, the balance between pain and joy shapes how you see things, how you act, and how you feel. One powerful truth is that joy is something inside you, not just a faraway idea. Even when life gets tough, you can still find joy deep within you. This is especially true when you face really tough changes and challenges that transform your life.

I know it's possible that you might think that joy and pain can't exist together – just as how a gust of wind puts out a candle's flame. But it's not that simple. Joy isn't just a feeling that comes and goes based on good things happening. It's like a well of good feelings that's always there, even when things seem hard. Knowing that joy isn't just about what's happening around you will help you understand how to handle tough times.

When pain feels overwhelming, holding onto joy is how you take care of yourself. Losing someone, big changes, and really hard challenges can feel like they are taking over your life. At these times, remembering to keep joy alive is really important. Just like you'd find a safe place in a storm, holding onto joy can help you feel better when things seem really tough. Keeping hold of joy doesn't mean ignoring pain. It's a choice to feel happy even when things are tough. It's like trying to walk on a thin rope between two worlds – knowing you are in pain but also choosing not to let it control you completely. Pain might be there, but you don't have to let it take over your whole life. By choosing joy when things are tough, you show how strong you are and that you can find meaning even in really dark moments.

The choices you make are really important in this balance between joy and pain. Life can throw challenges at you that feel impossible, changes that shake your whole world. But even in this storm of change, you have the power to choose how you react. You can't control everything that happens, but you can control how you feel about it. Think of it like you are an artist with a paintbrush – you can choose to make your life more colorful by adding joy, even when things are hard.

Choosing not to let your emotions be controlled by what's happening around you is really empowering. Your feelings belongs to you, and your life is yours to live. Even when changes make things tough, you are the one who gets to decide how you respond. This isn't about ignoring pain or pretending it doesn't hurt. It's about knowing that pain doesn't have to be in charge of your life. When things are tough, choosing joy shows you are in control of your feelings.

Even though it might seem strange, holding onto joy when things are tough will help you in practical ways. Joy is a light that guides you through rough times. It helps you see things more clearly, so you can make better choices and find solutions even when everything seems confusing.

Joy also changes how you see things, holding onto joy doesn't mean ignoring pain or pretending everything is fine. Instead, it's about finding balance. It's okay to feel sad and to take time to heal, but it's also okay to find joy sometimes. This change in how you see things will help you grow and change, even when life is tough.

Joy isn't a fixed thing – it's something that needs care and attention, your joy grows when you focus on it. Doing things that make you happy, spending time with loved ones, and taking breaks to relax all help your joy grow.

In short, going through tough times while holding onto joy shows how strong you are. It's about choosing happiness over sadness, even when things feel really hard. This journey isn't about ignoring pain – it's about understanding that you have the right to be happy. Think of it as a flower that grows in difficult conditions – you can come out of challenges with joy, showing that you have hope and strength deep inside you.

Chapter 3

What Happens if we Run from Change?

"Just as ignoring a problem won't make it disappear, avoiding change only postpones the inevitable, often magnifying the issue over time."

Running away might seem to be a good idea in certain situations. Let's say you are resorting in the mountains, and you see a wild animal before it sees you. It's smart to quietly sneak away and leave the place. But sometimes, big changes happen in your life, and it might not be the best choice to just run away from them. Running away from your problems might work for a little while but you cannot keep running forever. If a change in your life makes you feel anxious, uncertain, or even causes some physical issues. At first, you might not want to face it and this might seem to be a smart thing to do – just ignore it for a little while. But you see, sooner or later, you will have to deal with the change. Unless it's not a big deal, you will need to address it before it becomes a bigger problem.

Look at it this way also, if for example your son starts acting in a way that's not like him. You think it's because he's a teenager and that's normal. Then you notice he's not doing his schoolwork, cleaning his room, or hanging out with friends – things he used to do. That's not typical behavior for him. You want to talk to him about it, but you know he might just roll his eyes at you. It's like talking to a wall sometimes. So, you decide to ignore the problem.

But then things get worse, your son spends most of his time alone in his room. He wears headphones and avoids looking at you. He gets into a fight at school and his grades start dropping. You might think it's just a phase he'll get over. But this is a situation that needs attention. Your child is either asking for help in a not-so-obvious way, or he might be in danger. It's time to address the issue before it gets worse and affects him even more.

Ignoring change often makes a situation worse, some consequences of ignoring change are as follows

Stagnation:

Avoiding change always looks easy, but it comes with its own price. When we stick to the same old routine, even if it's not making us happy, we're essentially standing still while time marches on. Can you imagine being stuck in a never-ending loop, where life becomes motionless and unexciting? Choosing to avoid change always feel comfortable at first, but in the long run, it creates a feeling of dissatisfaction because our lives can lose their vitality if we don't embrace change. The discomfort we feel when we face change is like the initial splash when you jump into a pool – it might be chilly, but it wakes you up and keeps the water fresh.

Missed Opportunities:

Change often comes with doors opening to new opportunities. I want you to see life as a big adventure park. Every change is a new ride waiting for you to hop on. But when you avoid change, it means you have decided to walk past all those exciting rides without giving them a shot. You are missing out on chances to learn, to grow, and to achieve things you might not have even imagined.

Think about it – when you avoid change, you are saying no to learning new skills, meeting new people, and having amazing experiences. This is you saying no to a road trip because you are used to your usual route. But that road trip could lead you to incredible places you have never seen before. Embracing change is a decision to explore those new roads and discover the hidden gems they hold.

You Live with Regret and Stress:

You should never regret what you didn't do. That's what happens when you fail to address change. You simply allow it to happen and let the chips fall where they may. What if you had taken action instead? You might have stopped an unfortunate change or even reversed it. What would your life have been like? Don't live with this regret. Embrace change and do what you can to make your situation better.

There's also a lot of stress with not tackling change. If the change is still there, constantly in your face, it can cause chronic stress. That's a condition linked to severe health problems and a situation that can be avoided.

Resentment:

Have you ever seen someone zoom ahead in a race while you are stuck at the starting line? Avoiding change can make us feel that way – it make us feel left behind while others move forward. It's you watching everyone else get the spotlight while you are in the shadows. This leads to a sour feeling of resentment and unhappiness. When we resist change and see others thriving, it's easy to feel envy. We might think, "Why is everyone else getting ahead while I'm stuck here?"

Loss of Self-Confidence:

Avoiding change quietly chips away at your self-confidence. It's you saying to yourself "I can't handle this new situation." Just think of it as if life were a series of tests. Each time you face a new challenge, it's an opportunity to prove your skills. But when you run away from change, it's you skipping the test and believing you will never be able to pass it. Every change is a chance to learn and grow, If you avoid change, you miss out on building yourself. This leads to self-doubt over time – like forgetting who you are and your real strengths and thinking you are not capable of tackling new challenges. Embracing change means believing in yourself and realizing you are much more capable than you thought.

Lack of Fulfillment:

Imagine life as a book with different chapters, avoiding change is like re-reading the same chapter over and over. Sure, it might be familiar, but it also gets repetitive and less exciting. When you stick to what you know, your life becomes like a comfortable, well-worn path in a park. But while that path might be easy, it might not lead you to the breathtaking view at the top of the hill. When we avoid change, we're essentially saying no to new experiences, challenges, and adventures. These are the things that infuse our lives with a sense of fulfillment and excitement. It's like choosing to eat the same meal every day instead of trying new flavors. The routine might be convenient, but it lacks the thrill of discovering something new and delicious.

Disconnection from Others:

Picture change as a train station with trains heading to different destinations. When we embrace change, we hop on a train and move forward with others. But when we avoid change, we might stand at the station watching those trains leave without us. This can make us feel disconnected from the people around us who are on different journeys. As life moves forward, change is the glue that keeps our relationships in sync. But when we resist change, this is us being out of step with everyone else's dance. Our friends might have new stories to share, but we're still stuck in the old chapter. This disconnection makes one feel standing still while the world moves on.

You Could Be Signing Your Death Warrant:

Imagine that you haven't always eaten foods that promote health and wellness. You know this yet you have made no attempt to embrace a healthy diet over the years. The problem is that you are not a kid anymore, you don't have that unique metabolism that allows you to eat whatever you like and stay healthy.

Perhaps because of your diet your doctor tells you about all the negative changes that have been happening to your body over the last few years. He lays out a regimen of dietary changes, exercise, stress reduction practices, and medication to help you become healthy again. He mentions that your smoking and drinking addictions are certainly not helping your situation. This is, unfortunately, a common situation these days. I assure you that if you decide to ignore all he has said just because you don't like the change in routine, exercise and diet then be prepared to sign your death warrant soon.

Several ways we run away from change

Change will always happen in life, and it will most times stir up several emotions ranging from excitement to apprehension. Despite its inevitability, many people resort to diverse strategies to evade its grasp. While these tactics might offer a fleeting sense of relief, they will hinder personal growth and impede the potential for positive transformation. Let's see several ways people run away from change:

Denial and Evasion of Reality: In the face of impending change, some individuals prefer to deny its existence. They may downplay its significance or completely ignore the signs that change is occurring. This self-imposed ignorance creates a false sense of security but ultimately obstructs their ability to address the change in a constructive manner.

Procrastination and Delaying Action: The act of postponing the inevitable is a common approach to dealing with change. People often believe that delaying addressing a situation will lead to its resolution. However, this procrastination often amplifies stress and anxiety, resulting in missed opportunities for adaptation and growth.

Comfort Zone Preservation: The allure of the comfort zone is powerful. Many individuals are drawn to the familiar and the routine, finding solace in their current circumstances. This reluctance to step beyond what is known prevents them from embracing the discomfort that accompanies change, even if it signifies bypassing potential benefits.

Putting the Blame on Others: Sometimes, people like to say that problems are not their fault, but someone else's. This way, they don't have to take responsibility for making things better. They don't have to deal with the changes they need to make in themselves.

Getting Distracted and Running Away: People can keep themselves busy with work, games, or other things so they don't have to deal with changes. This can help them feel better for a little while, but it doesn't solve the real problems or help them move forward.

Thinking Too Much and Not Doing: Sometimes, thinking too much about every little thing can stop people from doing anything at all. It's good to think, but if they think too much, they might not do anything, and that keeps them from changing and growing.

Holding On to the Past: People might really appreciate the way things used to be, and that's okay. But if they only think about the past and don't want things to change, they might miss out on good things in the future. Being stuck in the past can stop them from trying new things.

Trying to Be Perfect: Some people want everything to be just right before they do something. They think that if everything is perfect, nothing will go wrong. But waiting for everything to be perfect can make them miss out on chances to change and learn.

Always Thinking Bad Things: If people always think that things will turn out bad, they might not even try to change. They might think, "What's the use? It won't work anyway." This kind of thinking can make them feel bad and stop them from getting better.

Scared of Failing and Taking Risks: Some people are so scared of failing that they don't even try. They'd rather stay the same than take a chance and fail. But if they don't try, they won't know if they can succeed.

Comparing Yourself to Others: If people look at others and think they are better at changing, they might feel bad about themselves. They might think they are not good enough. This can make it hard for them to change and become better.

Relying Too Much on Habits: Doing the same things every day can make people feel safe and comfortable. But if those things aren't helping, they might need to change. It's like always wearing the same shoes even if they are too small - it doesn't help in the long run.

In conclusion, the multitude of strategies employed to avoid change may provide temporary respite, but they obstruct personal development and stifle growth opportunities. Acknowledging these evasion tactics empowers you to make informed choices, step beyond your comfort zones, and embrace change as a catalyst for positive transformation. The realization that these avoidance mechanisms impede personal progress encourages a conscious shift toward embracing change as an avenue for growth and self-discovery.

Section Two

Common Changes We Face

In the course of our lives, we come across a multitude of changes, both subtle and transformative. These changes are an integral aspect of the human experience, shaping our personal adventures in ways that often catch us by surprise. From the earliest stages of life to the later years, change weaves its intricate threads through every chapter of our existence. The changes we encounter form the very design of our lives. They challenge us, transform us, and mold us into individuals with the capacity to adapt, learn, and grow.

Chapter 4

Financial Changes

"Lacking adaptation to new financial realities can lead to prolonged financial hardship, debt accumulation, and damage to credit scores, impacting overall well-being."

Losing your job or having income drastically reduced shakes up everything. The stability of daily life suddenly vanishes. Regular expenses like rent and utilities stay the same, but the money to cover them, shrinks. This new reality feels scary and uncertain. But resisting change by clinging to old comfortable spending habits only prolongs the pain. Adaptation is required to create a new kind of stability.

At first, it may seem impossible to imagine a different lifestyle with less money coming in. Major downsizing of housing, activities, and entertainment spending must happen. Credit card debt accumulates quickly when trying to maintain the status quo. Tension and blame rise within families as hopes fade of returning to how things used to be. Anxiety is constant without the predictability of a regular paycheck. Over time, the health consequences build through poor nutrition, inadequate sleep, and stress. Well-being deteriorates without income stability, but summoning energy for self-care feels impossible when just surviving day-to-day.

Lacking sufficient emergency savings worsens the disruption because existing reserves get consumed rapidly by ongoing expenses, removing all financial flexibility. Interest payments accumulate and soon minimum credit card payments erase any remaining room for financial freedom. As time passes without adaptation, life spirals downward on all fronts, I mean the going down of your physical, mental, relational and financial life.

Yes indeed, major financial change can severely damage stability unless habits evolve to match the new reality. Avoiding this adaptation by clinging to the past only makes the situation worse. With courage and creativity, a new kind of stability can be built through resourcefulness and saving. But resisting change means prolonging disruption rather than recovering equilibrium.

Some Major Consequences of Refusing to Accept a Change in Finances in good faith includes:

Prolonged Financial Hardship: If you fail to adapt spending to match lower income, financial hardship drag on indefinitely. Rejecting reality keeps money problems alive much longer. Avoidance wastes the little resources left rather than adjusting to live within reduced means.

Damaged Credit and Debt: Denying the need to downsize also leads to reliance on credit cards and loans. Debt accumulates at alarming speed with no plan to pay it off. Missed payments hurt credit scores. Interest builds up. Before long, you are dug into a deep financial hole.

Lost Savings and Assets: Additionally, refusing to downsize assets such as cars and homes to fit the new reality can be disastrous. Holding onto unaffordable things drains savings rapidly. Eventually, homes go into foreclosure or vehicles get repossessed. These outcomes are traumatic and create long-term damage.

Strained Relationships: Not accepting change also harms close relationships, Resentment brews as strained finances affect loved ones. Blame gets tossed around rather than working together. Major money conflicts can fracture families permanently.

Health Declines: The health toll of prolonged financial stress is measurable, it includes: anxiety, poor diet, and inadequate healthcare damage wellbeing. Energy is sapped. Focus narrows to just survival. Motivation for self-care fades when finances look hopeless.

Depression: In fact, refusing to accept new financial constraints often leads to depression. Feeling powerless breeds despair and robs life of meaning. Self-esteem suffers. Instead of adjusting, we withdraw into isolation and bitterness.

Missed Opportunities: Adapting spending opens up new opportunities that soberness reveals. Finding creative ways to meet needs on less income builds character and wisdom. But stubbornly denying change means missing chances to help others and redefine priorities.

Trauma and Anxiety: Additionally, resisting major money change increases trauma and uncertainty. The endless freefall of avoidance is more psychologically damaging than embracing limitation. Living in financial chaos heightens anxiety. It feels safer to accept reality.

Loss of Purpose: Without acceptance, daily life also becomes aimless and purposeless. Just surviving day-to-day replaces striving for meaningful goals. Getting stuck in bitterness warps perspective and sacrifices the future. Life revolves around past losses rather than present possibilities.

Damaged Self-Worth: Finally, refusing to accept a new financial situation harms self-image and confidence. You begin to feel ashamed and inadequate rather than adaptable and resilient. But in fact, how you respond to adversity reveals your inner strength. Acceptance is brave and wise.

How financial changes lead to depression when not handled well:

John's Job Loss

John was let go from his company after many loyal years, there. It shocked and devastated him. He had steadily moved up over time to a well-paying manager role that supported his family's comfortable lifestyle. Now at age 45, he felt too old to find a similar job. His industry was dying out anyway. John's whole career path and identity was tied up in this company.

Even worse, John then discovered his financial advisor had stolen all the retirement savings he had invested over the last decade. Just like that, it was all gone in a fraud scheme. John was left with only a small checking account buffer and a mortgage he could no longer afford. His safety net evaporated through no fault of his own.

At first, John was in denial. He refused to significantly cut spending or make major life changes. He clung desperately to normalcy, despite having little income. John drained the last dollars from savings to keep up old habits. He believed a fantastic new job would come along soon to restore everything as it was.

But as weeks turned to months with no income or interviews, John's denial shifted to despair. His family started resenting his refusal to adapt. John isolated himself at home, paralyzed by anxiety and bitterness. He started drinking to cope. His mind clouded with dark thoughts about the future.

Finally, John's brother insisted he sees a therapist. Though resistant at first, he slowly opened up about losing all hope. The therapist helped him realize rejecting reality was harming everyone. With support, John began the difficult process of letting go, downsizing, and reimagining their family's lifestyle. It felt liberating to accept the truth, even though very painful.

Once John stopped fighting the new circumstances, he regained a sense of control and purpose. He discovered simple joys and ways to contribute without much money. John realized his family valued him, not his paycheck. He took baby steps each day, rebuilding self-esteem and resilience. Their new life lacked frills but abounded in what mattered most.

Though the intense pain and despair returned in waves for years, John no longer drowned in them. He learned to ride them out and recognize the beauty ahead.

A Word from My Heart

When life throws you a curveball and everything changes overnight, it's natural to want to resist. You cling to the past, to what you know and find comfortable. But denying reality only locks you in a prison of your own making. Fighting the inevitable lengthens the suffering rather than lighting the way forward.

I know right now it feels overwhelming. The sudden loss of stability rocks you to the core. Your mind screams this is unfair and unacceptable. You desperately long to turn back time and restore what was taken. Adapting to a new normal seems unimaginable when you are still in shock. But you have inner reserves of courage, even when hidden from view. Take heart that this painful transition will not last forever. Though shrouded by darkness now, you will emerge wiser and more resilient. Acceptance is the first step, though the hardest.

Do not despair that life as you knew it has ended. A new life awaits discovery, one perhaps less materially rich but brimming with meaning. Have faith that you will create fresh purpose beyond current circumstances. For now, focus only on making it through today. And tomorrow, begin again. Cherish your loved ones, and let them carry you when strength fails. Their loyalty is a lifeline to cling to amidst the churning waters. You need not walk this road alone. Together, build a new stability rooted in appreciation for all you still have.

Free yourself from roles and titles that once defined you, but now constrict growth. You are not your job, possessions, or achievements. You are far greater - a repository of talents waiting to shine. Shed the past version of yourself to call forth your full potential.

Surrender the quest to control everything. Grant yourself grace to be human. Perfection is the enemy of progress. Be patient and take small steps. Each lesson makes you wiser. Each breath builds courage to face what lies ahead.

Soon, the deafening noise of resentment and regret will fade. In its place, the quiet joy of self-discovery grows. You realize how superficial past priorities ring hollow now. In simplicity, you reconnect to your essence.

This is not the end, but a new beginning. Do not dwell on setbacks, but redemption. Each sunrise offers opportunity to reinvent and renew. As time passes, wounds transform into wisdom. Your transformation will inspire others.

So dry your tears. Stand tall again. You are the hero of your own life, now more than ever as you conquer fear and embrace change. Your finest chapter has yet to be written. The story continues, more glorious than you can yet imagine.

Chapter 5

Career/Business Changes

"In the face of career transitions, resilience, adaptability, and purpose become tools to navigate the journey, reminding us that growth is not confined to a single role but a continuous pursuit."

One of the most difficult yet frequent changes people navigate over a lifetime is in their work. As the years go on, most careers transform dramatically, forcing people to adapt or switch paths entirely. Though deeply challenging, this experience is near universal.

Many times external forces drives this "Business and Career" change against people's will. New technologies rise up that automate or render obsolete the skills people rely on. Or economic meltdown shuts entire industries, leaving people stranded. A global pandemic, political upheaval, or corporate merger can suddenly upset professions.

In other cases, the shift comes from within because as people grow and evolve through life's phases, the jobs they once loved no longer stir their passions. Skills people worked hard to perfect now seem outdated and limiting. Responsibilities that energized people in their 20s feel stale and unfulfilling by their 40s. They crave new horizons.

Whatever the cause, stark career transitions force people to confront deep questions of identity and purpose. So much of how people see themselves gets tied up in their professional titles and achievements. Letting go means untethering from a reputation and status they treasure. Admitting an industry or job no longer fits comes with shame and disappointment. The thought of starting from scratch in a new field overwhelms. Yet refusing career change out of fear breeds regret. Clinging to the past sacrifices future potential. With time, most careers demand reinvention in order for people to stay aligned with their evolving goals and values. Each transition, however unwanted initially, brings rejuvenation and room for growth.

While humbling and anxiety-provoking, overcoming inertia to make a career change might become one of people's proudest accomplishments. It represents choosing courage over complacency, daring to envision a more fulfilling path even amidst uncertainty. The process of shedding one identity to uncover a truer self builds character and wisdom. By embracing the opportunities hidden within change, people's working lives transform into journeys rather than traps. With resilience, adaptability, and purpose, people can navigate the inevitable ups and downs of any long-term career. Work change remains painful yet liberating, reminding people that they are not defined by a single role or skill, but by their inner resolve to keep growing.

Some negative consequences that will be experienced when someone is unable to accept this Business/Career change in good fate are:

Prolonged Unhappiness: Refusing to accept the need for career change often dooms people to prolonged unhappiness. By clinging to roles that no longer fit, they sacrifice their engagement and passion for work. As the mismatch widens over time, dissatisfaction festers into resentment, apathy, and burnout.

Deteriorating Skills: Additionally, refusing change in careers where skills become outdated leads to gradual deskilling. People fall further behind modern standards the longer they resist retraining. Their value in the job market plummets as competence deteriorates.

Lost Opportunities: Dodging necessary career change also leads people to miss new opportunities taking shape around them. By stubbornly holding onto the past, they fail to position themselves to thrive in emerging industries and roles. Missed chances accumulate.

Alienation: Resisting change also takes social and emotional tolls. People who refuse to adapt often isolate themselves as colleagues move forward. Clinging to the past breeds bitterness that strains work relationships.

Eroded Self-Worth: Denial of career change chips away at self-confidence over time. Being left behind by progress heightens feelings of inadequacy and low self-esteem. Admitting skills are obsolete feels devastating.

Financial Hardship: On a practical level, failure to change careers proactively often results in reactive job loss later, creating income disruption. Sudden unemployment forces a change without sufficient planning and preparation. Savings get depleted reacting to crisis.

I believe you can now see that severe consequences emerge across all aspects of life when people cannot accept major career and business changes. Mental health suffers, relationships strain, skills atrophy, and financial instability results. With support and courage, people can take charge of necessary reinvention rather than become its victim.

Chapter 6

Health Challenges

"Amidst the distressing turmoil of health challenges, the individual grapples with a loss of vitality, purpose, and connection, navigating a path where each day's triumphs are measured in moments of survival."

Life-altering illness or disability unleashes ripple effects that undermine every domain of life. Physical decline sets off a distressing downward spiral that impacts work, relationships, finances, emotions, and sense of purpose.

When our bodies can no longer perform as we expect them to, independence and self-reliance get stripped away. Activities that previously brought joy become limited or eliminated. We require help with basic functions like movement, hygiene, and household duties - painful blows to pride and privacy. Caregiver burdens breed guilt, though their support is essential. Isolation rises as weakened mobility keeps us housebound.

Financially, health conditions often force leaving beloved careers permanently. Lost income just as medical bills accumulate causes huge stress. Few can afford 24/7 home care, making institutionalization the only option over time. Long developed professional skills and achievements feel wasted when health excludes us from the workforce. Self-esteem takes a major hit.

Of course the physical symptoms themselves inflict misery - chronic pain, fatigue, nausea, shortness of breath, seizures, and more. Disease disrupts sleep, compounding physical and mental distress. Following strict treatment regimens and eliminating pleasant things like favorite foods become oppressive burdens. Endless medical interventions and procedures come to dominate life.

Mentally, unexpected health declines provoke tidal waves of grief, fear, and bitterness. We mourn vibrant abilities and futures snatched away, often permanently. Anxiety swirls about whether more loss lies ahead, as some conditions degenerate steadily over time. Shortened life expectancy haunts the thoughts of those with terminal diagnoses. The enormity of it all plunges even optimism into depression and despair.

Socially, health challenges also distance us from healthy friends and family who cannot relate. We stop participating in shared activities that highlight limitations and trigger envy. Conversations become dominated by monotonous discussion of symptoms and treatments, isolating us further when others tire of constant health-talk. They retreat, leaving us feeling excluded.

I need you to understand that a declining health robs life of vibrancy and purpose. Surviving becomes the priority, displacing goals and pleasures that provide meaning. Time gets measured from one medical procedure or hospitalization to the next. Whatever future remains looks defined by steady disability and decline. Once vibrant dreams and plans for the future seem ridiculous in light of physical frailty. The window of possibility closes to a small aperture focused solely on enduring. Our sense of identity shrivels down to that of a condition rather than a complete person.

Negative consequences of refusing to accept health changes, look on the bright side and move on

Negative Thoughts Make Things Worse:

When health issues come up, it's normal for your feelings to be affected. Feeling sad, frustrated, or even angry is common when you are not feeling well. If you don't deal with these emotions, they can make things even harder. You might start to feel as though there's no hope and that things will never get better. These negative feelings can lead you to make choices that aren't good for your well-being, similar to not taking care of yourself properly. And if you keep thinking about these negative emotions, it can be tough to see that there's a chance to heal and grow.

Losing Focus on Healing:

When you are dealing with health problems, it's easy to only think about the hard parts and the pain. You might get so caught up in the difficulties that you forget that you could actually get better. It's important to remember the things that still bring you joy and happiness, like spending time with people you care about or doing things that make you happy. When you forget about the potential to heal and only think about the tough stuff, you could end up suffering for longer and missing out on chances to get better.

Not Accepting Help:

Dealing with health issues can sometimes make you feel alone. You might not want to ask for help from others because you want to be independent. But shutting people out can actually make things worse. Accepting help from friends, family, and doctors can give you the support you need. When you share what you are going through, you won't feel so alone. And the people around you will have a chance to help you. It can be hard to let others see you vulnerable, but asking for support can really help you manage your health challenges.

Only Seeing the Bad Stuff:

When your health isn't great, it's easy to only focus on the tough parts. You might be in pain or feeling uncomfortable, and that can make everything else seem unimportant. But even when you are dealing with health issues, there are still good things in life. You have people who care about you, happy moments, and chances to learn and grow. If you start paying attention to these positive things, it can actually make you feel better overall.

Feeling Jealous of Others:

Comparing yourself to others is something everyone does, but it can be tough when you are not feeling well. Seeing other people who are healthy and happy can make you feel jealous or even upset. You might wonder why you have to deal with health problems while others seem to be doing just fine. But remember, everyone has their own challenges. Instead of focusing on what you don't have, try to focus on your own journey and find support from people who understand what you are going through.

Worrying About the Future:

When health issues are ongoing, it's easy to worry about what's going to happen next. The uncertainty of the future, combined with worries about how your health will affect your life, can make you feel anxious and stressed. This is when having things such as faith or a sense of purpose can be really helpful. They can give you a sense of stability and direction, helping you stay focused on what's happening right now. Mindfulness practices can also keep you grounded and prevent your thoughts from going to dark and scary places.

Ignoring Treatment:

It can be tough to stick to treatment plans when you are dealing with health issues. You might not be sure if what the doctor recommends will actually work. But ignoring your self-care and not following the treatments can make your symptoms worse. Remember, doctors know what they are talking about. Listening to them and doing what they say is an important part of managing your health challenges. If you are unsure, don't hesitate to ask questions or get a second opinion.

Forgetting About Your Feelings:

When you are not feeling well, it's easy to only think about your physical health. But your emotional well-being is important too. Feeling sad, frustrated, or even angry is natural when you are dealing with health problems. Ignoring these emotions can make you feel disconnected and overwhelmed. It's important to address your feelings and find ways to express them. Spending time doing things you enjoy, talking to people you trust, or even seeking help from a counselor can all make a big difference in how you manage your health.

Money Problems:

Health issues can affect your finances, especially if they stop you from working. You might feel proud and not want to ask for help or change your spending habits. But not facing financial realities can lead to more stress, debt, and overall unhappiness. It's okay to ask for help when you need it and make smart choices about your finances. Accepting assistance and making changes to your spending habits can help you manage your health challenges in a better way.

In conclusion, the way you react to health challenges have a big impact on how well you manage them. By recognizing the problems that negative thoughts, isolation, and ignoring self-care will cause, you can make things better. It's important to accept support, remember both the good and tough parts of life, and take care of your emotional, physical, and spiritual well-being. With a positive and empowered approach, you will be able to navigate health challenges in a way that helps you grow, become more resilient, and find renewed purpose in life.

Here is the story of a woman who fell victim to this dilemma

A story is told of a lady, for 20 years, Jane thrived as an engineer, renowned for her intellect and work ethic. She took pride in being fully self-sufficient. Jane's career was the cornerstone of her identity. At just 48 though, early onset dementia robbed Jane of her formidable mental capacities over a few short years. She could no longer perform professional duties that once came easily. Her whole sense of self-worth crumbled. Jane refused to accept having to leave her career. She hid her growing confusion and mistakes, dangerously clinging to an illusion of competence. Coworkers' concern seemed like pity, which Jane resented bitterly. Being isolated by pride, Jane stopped calling close friends who could have helped emotionally. She dwelled on perceived injustices of the disease and spent hours anxiously ruminating about the future rather than enjoying the present. Despite Jane's growing cognitive impairment, she insisted on living alone. But she started neglecting health, often forgetting medications and meals. Bills went unpaid as finances became unmanageable.

Yet Jane refused help, believing it implied weakness. Her mental and physical health spiraled lower until emergency hospitalization was required. Lost independence was traumatic on top of her existing anguish. Consumed by self-pity, Jane stopped fighting the undertow pulling her down. She gave up psychological and speech therapies as pointless. Isolation increased in the care home as Jane rejected social activities.

While Jane's diagnosis was unfair, fighting it now worsened her condition. By clinging to the past rather than accepting her evolving abilities, Jane lost precious time to make the most of her present.

With support and adaption, contentment was still possible. But bitterness obscured this truth, preventing Jane from finding peace.

Chapter 7

Relationships Changes

"Relationships, like the seasons, have their own ebb and flow, and while the pain of loss is undeniable, embracing the natural evolution of bonds allows us to welcome kindred spirits that enrich our journey anew."

One of the most universal yet painful parts of life is relationships changing over time, this means friends, romantic partners, even family who are once close to us inevitably drift away or exit our lives entirely. Though this is devastating, this loss is part of the natural evolution process of life.

In life as the years pass, our interests and priorities transform based on life experiences, the activities, values, and conversations that once nourished our spirits begins to lose relevance. We discover new passions our old social circle cannot relate to. Communication becomes strained when we have less in common. Shared history alone cannot preserve connections without ongoing mutual investment.

Our focus shifts too as we enter new life chapters. Career ambitions demand more hours at the office. New parents devote energy toward raising children. Retirees take on volunteer projects and hobbies. Friends accustomed to our past role feel neglected in the shuffle of changing priorities and limited time. Envy arises when it seems we pour passion into new relationships instead of evenly dividing our diminished attention.

Physical distance also accelerates relationship demise as well, because when life takes friends or partners to different cities, connection relies on effort. Face-to-face interactions get replaced by digital catch-ups. Yet despite good intentions, friends moving away fades bonds over time. Out of sight out of mind kicks in when life's demands consume us, I tell you the truth, long distance communication drops lower on the priority list without the ease of local proximity.

Romantic relationships face particularly steep challenges from diverging personal growth. Have you not noticed that the passionate couple who were joined at the hip in their twenties may find little common ground a decade later? People evolve and mature at different paces. What one person values and envisions for the future no longer aligns with the other person as it once did. The exciting chemistry that initially bonded them fades over years of complacency, but I want to quickly state here that partners must rekindle intimacy or accept going separate ways.

Of course, letting go of relationships that are once so meaningful feels painful and devastation as I said earlier. We mourn the loss of shared experiences, emotional support, laughter, and belonging that we once relied on. Anger, resentment, and sadness seems to emerge as changes beyond our control disrupt treasured bonds.

Yet resisting natural evolution simply prolongs unfulfilling relationships past their expiration date. We must find the courage to let go with grace when connections no longer nourish our spirit. Cherish fond memories and the role people played for a season, but respect when it is time to move in new directions. Though not what we would have chosen, accepting relational changes frees us to seek kindred spirits that uplift this next chapter of our journey. For all relationships, change remains inevitable. But by embracing it with maturity and faith, we adapt to love and be loved at each turn.

Here are some potential negative effects of being unable to accept relationship changes:

Long term unhappiness: Refusing to let go of unfulfilling relationships keeps us stuck in dissatisfaction rather than seeking more compatible connections.

Stunted personal growth: Clinging to stale relationships prevents us from developing new interests and passions that have emerged from life changes. We limit our own evolution.

Resentment: Desperately holding on breeds resentment as we try to force something that no longer fits. We may envy new relationships as old ones deteriorate.

Loss of identity: Basing our entire identity on one relationship leaves us rudderless when it changes. We have to rebuild self-concept from within rather than relying on a partner for validation.

Time wasted: Remaining in lifeless relationships steals time that could be better invested in more promising bonds. Missed opportunities with new kindred spirits accumulate.

Social isolation: When we cannot move on, we distance ourselves from wider social circles to exclusively invest in a failing relationship. This narrows our support network.

Clouded judgment: An inability to accept relationship changes makes realistic assessment of compatibility impossible. We idealize poor fits rather than acknowledging incompatibility.

Mental health issues: Clinging to relationships that are changing can breed anxiety, depression and obsessive behaviors. Letting go frees us to find emotional stability again.

In a nutshell, the inability to gracefully accept relationship changes locks us into pain, stunted growth, and missed opportunities. With courage and maturity, we can embrace change as opening doors to new connections and self-discovery.

Chapter 8

Family Changes

"Family connections, a bedrock of stability through life's journey, evolve and change, teaching us that embracing the ebb and flow of relationships with understanding strengthens our bonds."

I've learned that in life, our family connections give us stability to handle life's ups and downs. The love they give us no matter what, helps us through good and bad times. We rely on our family to be there for us, even when they are far away. So it can be sad when family relationships change as years go by. We might want things to always be the same. But understanding this reality as we grow up helps us change and adapt together.

Big changes start when we are kids, new brothers or sisters join the family. Our routines and attention shift to include them. When parents separate, it changes our home. Getting used to two new homes can be hard emotionally. Other tough things like moving away from friends and cousins also change our young lives. But meeting new people and learning to stay in touch even if we're far away makes us strong.

As we become adults, family members move for new jobs. Some move nearby, while others go to different parts of the country. We see them less, and it's not the same. Even if we want to, we don't talk as much without seeing each other every day. Big moments in life happen from far away.

But you know what? Holding onto good memories and family stories keeps our connections alive, even when we're apart. Family members stay in our hearts, no matter where they are in life.

Inside families, relationships between people change too. Friends we were super close to as kids might not be as close as we grow up. Small arguments can become big problems without the fun of playing together every day. Even holiday times together might feel tense sometimes.

Accepting these changes with understanding, not bitterness, stops big separations. Forgiving things that happened in the past and finding things we have in common keeps our bonds strong. At the same time, new parts of the family form when people get married or have kids. Welcoming step-parents, in-laws, and grandkids adds more love, but also different opinions to balance. Let the new parts of the family grow while still caring for what was there before.

Finally, adult children slowly become caregivers as their parents get older. Making choices about their health and money can feel strange after all those years when they took care of us. Sometimes, they don't want help because they are proud. But remembering how they always put us first helps us now take care of them as they get older. Getting used to new roles takes time.

Through everything, love keeps families together. People come and go, but our shared history and values keep us strong. By bravely accepting each change as a chance to grow, families get closer over time. What stays is the feeling that we belong no matter what.

Now let us see some negative effects of not accepting family changes gracefully:

Stubbornness Damages Close Ties:

When family relationships evolve and change, it's important to accept these changes wholeheartedly. Refusing to let go of the past due to fear or stubbornness can poison what were once strong bonds. This lack of acceptance often leads to feelings of resentment and isolation, creating cracks in relationships that were once unbreakable.

Separation Anxiety over Moving:

Imagine you are a young adult excited to explore new horizons after college. However, if your parents resist this change and guilt-trip you for pursuing your dreams, it can have negative consequences. Manipulative tactics, such as threatening to withdraw support, can replace celebration with control. This refusal to accept your independence can strain the family dynamic.

Fractured Sibling Connections

Siblings who shared childhood memories can find their relationship strained when their adult beliefs clash. If they are unable to accept and understand each other's differing views, their connection might weaken. Instead of cherishing their unique perspectives, not embracing these changes can lead to judgment and trust issues, dividing what once united them.

Excluding New Family Members:

When new family members join the fold through marriage or other bonds, not making space for them can cause negative effects. When longer-standing family members don't accept these newcomers, a sense of exclusion can grow. Failing to reshape traditions and rituals to include everyone can create a divide, making the new members feel like outsiders.

Resenting Caregiver Responsibilities:

As adults, when you are asked to step into caregiving roles for aging parents, resistance can lead to strained relationships. Rejecting this change due to a desire for personal freedom might result in bitterness. Instead of empathizing with your parents' needs, this refusal can lead to complaints, creating a less supportive environment during a time of transition.

Pride Hindering Accepting Help:

Parents facing aging-related challenges might resist receiving assistance due to pride. Not accepting the help they need can accelerate their decline and contribute to feelings of isolation. If adult children are met with resistance when they try to offer support, it can lead to strained family relationships and emotional distance.

Divorce Battles Hurting Children:

In the aftermath of divorce, if parents continue to harbor hostility and fail to adjust their behavior, it can negatively affect their children. Being caught in the middle of their ongoing disputes can create a stressful environment. When parents prioritize their personal battles over their children's well-being, it erodes trust and emotional stability.

Toxicity from Unwillingness to Adapt:

When family members refuse to adapt to changes and new circumstances, toxicity can seep into relationships. Failing to acknowledge that families evolve over time can result in resentment and isolation. Clinging to old roles and relationships instead of embracing change can lead to division and weaken the family's foundation.

Empathy and Flexibility to Build Stronger Bonds:

Recognizing the negative consequences of not accepting family changes underscores the importance of empathy and flexibility. Accepting transitions with understanding and open-mindedness is vital for nurturing strong bonds within the family. By embracing change and adjusting to new phases of life together, families can maintain their closeness and resilience even in the face of challenges.

Chapter 9

Spirituality Changes

"As the church and our understanding of faith takes changing forms, Christ remains a constant companion on our spiritual journey, guiding us towards a dynamic relationship that transcends religious belief."

Understanding how change can happen in our Spiritual lives

As Christians, our faith and trust in God provides strength through all of life's ups and downs. God's love sustains us, even when our circumstances transform. Accepting these changes graciously keeps our spirit nourished.

Our relationship with God deepens and grows over a lifetime because as we mature in Christ, concrete childhood understandings of theology evolve into nuanced appreciation of Scripture's mysteries. We learn to balance tradition with contextual discernment under the Holy Spirit's guidance.

A major thing is that young believers sometimes discover a more passionate faith by exploring beyond the church of their upbringing. Their social justice values begins to synchronize more with progressive Christian churches focused on societal reform. Yet parents who cling to conservative tradition soon react with confusion, rather than appreciating their child's sincere spiritual progression and growth.

Sometime in line with growth, certain people begin to see that a certain traditional doctrine now limits a more authentic walk with Jesus. Their shifting perspectives causes grief, yet they must prayerfully follow Christ's call to new understanding. Their journey can inspire fellow believers experiencing doubts.

Relocating to a new place also isolates Christians from long-term church families and support systems. Finding a new congregation often take years in unfamiliar territories. Warm welcomes cannot instantly replace generations of collective worship and belonging.

Sometime prayerful study also reveal where traditional doctrines have been misapplied to justify prejudice, rather than grace. Christians realizing these flaws are compelled to realign faith with Jesus' inclusive ministry. This shift requires courage yet it frees us to love.

Through it all, Christ accompanies our spiritual journey as the church takes changing forms around us. By embracing the growth He ordains, our walk with God matures from being just a religious belief into dynamic relationship with the Lord.

Some Consequences of failing to accept Spiritual Changes

Refusing to accept necessary changes in the church can lead to negative consequences for believer over time, let us see some of it

Stagnation of Faith:

When Christians resist change in their faith community, their beliefs can become stagnant. Without a willingness to adapt and grow as life situations change, their faith can lose its vibrancy. The absence of growth in perspectives and practices can make their faith feel dull and unengaging.

Clinging to Traditions:

Holding onto strict traditions without considering new understanding can lead to problems. It can cause defensiveness and pride within the church community. Judging fellow believers who have different walks of faith can create divisions instead of promoting empathy and unity.

Fear of Change:

The fear of change can hinder the revitalization of one's faith. When people are afraid of embracing new ideas or approaches, their faith can become stagnant and unexciting. This fear prevents them from exploring new aspects of their spirituality.

Unhealthy Church Environments:

Staying in a church solely because of familiarity, despite it being unhealthy, can lead to spiritual fatigue. Engaging in hollow rituals without true fellowship can hinder one's spiritual growth. Bitterness can arise when important aspects like Biblical community, discipleship, and service are lacking.

Protection of Status:

Some resistance to change might come from a desire to protect one's status or influence within the church. However, prioritizing the status quo over needed changes can deter growth and repel potential new members. Refusing to update human doctrines can prevent alignment with God's evolving revelation.

Denial of Flaws:

Denying flaws in practices or interpretations can perpetuate harmful behavior. The fear of questioning tradition can prevent necessary examination and growth. The church as a whole remains unaware of issues requiring attention and guidance.

Isolation and Division:

Rejection of change can lead to isolation, as some members evolve differently from official stances. Doubters or those with differing views might feel pressured to conform or leave the church. Lack of diversity in perspectives can harm the entire congregation and hinder its growth.

Staying in Negative Environments:

Unwillingness to change churches in the face of negative situations can stall spiritual growth. Enduring discomfort without seeking more nourishing fellowship can hinder personal development. It's essential to find a church that aligns with one's beliefs and supports their spiritual journey.

In conclusion, refusing to accept necessary changes in the church can have detrimental effects on us - Christians and our spiritual growth. It's important to be open to new perspectives, adapt to evolving circumstances, and embrace changes that align with the core values of the faith and in line with bible teaching. This ensures that faith remains dynamic, supportive, and relevant in the lives of believers. Overall, the safety of resisting change is an illusion. Stagnant faith experiences no revival. What once brought life becomes an empty routine, I tell you the truth, seeking Jesus requires bravely stepping into new understandings that stretch vision but align with the Word.

Section Three

Embracing Change

Embracing change doesn't mean just accepting everything that comes our way. It's about having a positive attitude and being open to new experiences. Imagine you're trying a new sport. At first, it might feel strange, but with practice and a willingness to learn, you might end up enjoying it. Embracing change is like trying that new sport – you're giving yourself a chance to discover something amazing.

Change also teaches us important life lessons. It shows us that nothing stays the same forever, and that's okay. Just like the moon changes its shape in the sky, our lives go through different phases too. And just as the sun rises every day, change brings new beginnings and opportunities.

Chapter 10

Giving Change a Chance

"Change might seem daunting, but within it lies the power to craft something beautiful out of every challenge. You're the author of your own story, with the courage to shape your path."

Life, my friend, is a journey full of movement and surprises. But sometimes, we don't feel comfortable with the change. It is like going into something new and unknown. It's like stepping out of what we are used to and into something different. But let me tell you something important, in the middle of all these changes, there are lots of exciting things waiting for you to discover. It's a world where you can grow and succeed in ways you never thought possible.

We've all been there. We've faced changes that we didn't want or ask for. These changes can be scary and make us nervous. But even when things seem really tough, there are chances for good things to happen. What we often forget is that we have the power to make something beautiful out of every change that comes our way. Imagine how brave you are when you accept change. It's like standing at a crossroads – one path you know well, and the other is new and unknown. Choosing the new path takes a lot of courage. It's like being an actor and a writer at the same time. You have the power to decide how your story goes, based on what you really want in your heart.

Here's the truth, my friend, change will help you grow a lot, even when things feel uncertain, going forward and facing your fears will help you become a better person. Think about how a caterpillar becomes a butterfly. Change will take you from feeling worried to achieving great things.

Think about it – every new idea, every amazing creation, and every big step forward happened because people were open to change. The bravest explorers didn't avoid new places; they went to them and learned amazing things. Just like them, you can go through changes and discover new strengths, wisdom, and success. Don't let fear and regret stop you, they are just things that hold you back, just as an anchor on a ship. Instead, think of change as a guide, I mean as a compass that shows you where to go. Change can help you find happiness and success. Remember, it's not about getting rid of challenges; it's about using them to make your life better.

Deep inside you, there's a lot of strength. You can use this strength to face change and not be scared. Just like a bird doesn't fight the wind, you can let change guide you to new places.

Now is the time to give change a chance, let it help you become the best you can be. It can help you create your future in a way that makes you happy. Embrace it with open arms, knowing that it will bring you new experiences, growth, and joy. Stand tall, my friend, because you have the power to shape your life.

Now imagine there is a young student named Alex. He was once surrounded by the warmth of his parents' support, a covering of comfort. But one day, life took an unexpected turn – he lost his parents. This abrupt change shattered his world, leaving him in a sea of uncertainty.

Imagine this change as a sudden storm that struck his life. It was a storm that could have left him drowning in sorrow, lost in its torrential waves. However, Alex choses a different path. Instead of succumbing to despair, he decided to face this change head-on, like a ship navigating through rough waters.

At first, the storm brought hardships. The waves of grief threatened to overwhelm him. The sun of his carefree days was hidden behind the clouds of loss. But within Alex, a flame of determination flickered. He realized that this change, though painful, had the potential to be a catalyst for growth.

As he weathered the storm, Alex discovered the importance of perseverance. He learned to stand firm when the winds of challenge blew against him. Each day, he would wake up, put on his metaphorical armor of discipline, and march forward with unwavering resolve.

The journey wasn't easy. The storm had brought about financial struggles and emotional burdens. But Alex didn't let these obstacles deter him. He immersed himself in his studies, using education as an anchor to keep him steady amidst the chaos. Like a compass guiding him through uncharted waters, he used his academics to chart a course toward a brighter future. Through hard work and determination, Alex learned the art of discipline. He realized that success isn't handed on a silver platter; it's forged through sweat, dedication, and unyielding effort. Each day, he embraced the grind, much like a blacksmith shaping raw metal into a finely crafted blade.

As time went on, Alex's journey began to yield results. His hard work transformed into achievement. His perseverance led to growth. The storm that had once shaken his world was now the driving force behind his success. The hardships he faced became stepping stones toward a better future.

In this analogy, Alex is anyone who faces unexpected and challenging changes. His story shows us the transformative power of acceptance and hard work. Just like him, when life throws us into turbulent waters, we can choose to navigate through the storm. By embracing change, persevering through difficulties, and remaining disciplined in our pursuits, we can turn the darkest of storms into the winds that propel us toward success and a brighter future.

What we're saying is that you should give change a chance.

Don't turn away from change no matter how good or bad it is, instead, face it with courage, embrace it, not as an enemy, but as a teacher offering you new lessons. The path ahead might seem uncertain, but remember that within every change lies a chance for growth and transformation.

We all wish we had a magical time machine to rewind the clock and undo the changes we don't want. But alas, time machines are the stuff of dreams. The reality is that change has already happened, and the past is etched in stone. However, the future is like a canvas waiting for your brushstrokes, and you have the power to paint a masterpiece.

You might wonder, how can you possibly turn negative change into something beautiful? The answer lies in a seven-step system which are the core teachings of this section of this book. Prepare your heart as you study them, you are about to experience transformation like never before.

Chapter 11

Being Strong – Resilience

"Being strong doesn't mean just getting through change; it means doing well even when things are different. It's like a ship sailing on bumpy waters – it doesn't just survive the big waves, it learns to ride them and keep going."

Change as you have continually seen in this study always happens in life, and it can be good or tough. It can mess up your usual routines, plans, and how you feel stable. When things change, being strong and adaptable is really important. This helps us go through the tough times with courage, change your ways when you need to, and keep a positive attitude. Being strong doesn't mean just getting through change; it means doing well even when things are different. It's like a ship sailing on bumpy waters – it doesn't just survive the big waves, it learns to ride them and keep going. Being strong lets us handle tough times and come out of them even better.

Being strong helps you deal with change by being adaptable. Instead of not liking new things, you learn to be okay with them. This helps you change your plans and ideas when things are different. Instead of being stuck with what you wanted, you see change as a chance to try new things and find new good stuff. One great thing about being strong is thinking positively, instead of getting scared or unsure, strong people look at change with hope. They see problems as chances to get better and learn, not as things that are too big to handle. Being positive doesn't mean ignoring how hard things can be. It's a way of looking at problems that will make you want to keep trying and look for new ways to fix them.

When things change, we feel all kinds of emotions, like being worried or happy. Being strong helps us deal with these feelings in a good way. It's about knowing what we're feeling, where those feelings come from, and finding good ways to handle them. Instead of letting bad feelings take over, we learn to use them to do something good.

This doesn't mean you have to handle change by ourselves. It's okay to get help from people you trust, like friends, family, or teachers. When things are hard, talking to them and getting advice can make you feel better. Having people who listen and care makes us feel like we're not alone, and it helps us feel better about facing change.

Fixing Problems and Learning

Being strong also means you become good at fixing problems, I mean when things are hard, strong people see them as chances to learn and get better. They look at the situation, think of ways to fix it, and do something to make it better. This helps not only in that moment but also helps you be better at solving problems in the future. When you become strong and handle changes well, you can grow a lot as a person. Going through tough times, finding ways to fix things, and staying positive make you better in many ways. You become more confident, patient, and good at never giving up. This helps you deal with change now and in the future.

In life, when things change, being strong is really important. It's like the thread that holds everything together when things are different. Being strong means you see change as a way to grow, not as something scary. It helps you turn problems into chances to get better, tough times into learning moments, and not knowing what's next into a way to learn more about yourselves. By being strong, you don't just get through tough times; you come out of them even stronger, smarter, and more ready to face anything that comes our way.

Elements of Being Strong

Being Adaptable: Adapting is a personal skill that helps you deal with change. It means being okay with trying new things when your original plans don't work out. When you are open to new ideas, you can grow and come up with new ways of doing things. Flexibility is like your anchor when things change suddenly. It helps you change your path in a smooth way. Adapting makes you stronger and stops you from staying stuck. It also helps you see the good things that can come from change.

Having a Positive Attitude: Having a positive attitude is like having a strong power that you can use when things go wrong. When you see problems as something that will go away, you use your own strength to keep going. Being optimistic means thinking about problems as steps to get to your goals, not as things that stop you. It's not pretending things are perfect, but it's a way of thinking that gives you hope, makes you keep trying, and helps you find ways to fix problems. When you choose to be optimistic, you get the power to beat hard times and come out even stronger.

Managing Your Feelings: Managing your feelings means being in control of how you feel inside. It's okay to feel good or bad, and it's important to accept how you feel without blaming yourself. Knowing why you feel the way you do can help you understand why you react in certain ways. Learning good ways to handle your feelings, like being mindful and thinking about yourself, helps you deal with them in a healthy way. Instead of acting quickly because of your feelings, you can think about how to handle things better. This helps you become stronger and make better decisions.

Getting Support from Others: When things are tough, the people you know, like friends, family, and mentors, can help you a lot. When you talk to them about what you are going through, they can understand and care about you. They can give you good advice and different ideas that can help you solve problems. Knowing you are not alone can make you feel like you belong and help you feel better. Remembering that others are there for you reminds you that you can get through hard times together.

Solving Problems: Problem-solving is like having a toolbox to help you when things are hard. It's about looking at problems, finding out why they happen, and figuring out ways to fix them. When you are good at thinking and understanding, you can see problems coming. Making plans to solve problems helps you face them step by step. Problem-solving doesn't just help with today's problems, it makes you confident to handle future problems with smart thinking.

Taking Care of Yourself: Taking care of yourself is like building the base of your strength. Putting yourself first isn't being selfish, it's about keeping yourself safe and healthy. Doing things you enjoy, like exercising or being creative, makes you feel better. Taking time to rest and relax gives you energy. Taking care of yourself helps you stay strong even when things change a lot. When you look after yourself, you have more power inside you to handle tough times in a good way.

Being Strong by Building Resilience

Building resilience is you creating a powerful shield that protects you from the challenges of life. It's a step-by-step process that gives you the ability to handle difficulties with strength and grace. Let's take a closer look at the various steps you can take to develop resilience and become better equipped to face whatever comes your way.

Understanding Yourself: Start by diving deep into your own self. Recognize your strengths that have helped you overcome past problems and identify areas where you might need more support. Reflect on the challenges you have faced and the lessons you have learned from them. This self-reflection is like looking into a mirror that shows your inner strength. It helps you learn from your experiences and build on them.

Mindfulness and Acceptance: Practice mindfulness, which means being fully present in the moment. Accept the things that you can't change and understand that some parts of life are beyond your control. This practice reduces stress by focusing your attention on the present instead of worrying about the past or future. It helps you use your energy to deal with the things you can influence.

Learning and Growing: Adopt a growth mindset, a way of thinking that sees challenges as opportunities for personal growth. Every setback or difficulty teaches you something valuable about yourself and the world. Instead of thinking of obstacles as things that stop you, think of them as lessons that make you smarter. This mindset turns challenges into chances to become better.

Healthy Ways to Cope: Replace harmful ways of dealing with stress with better options. Instead of avoiding difficult feelings, face them directly. Do activities that help you relax and reduce stress, like exercising, meditating, writing in a journal, or doing things you enjoy. These actions let you release tension and feel balanced. Healthy ways to cope give you the tools to deal with problems in positive ways and feel better emotionally.

Connecting with Others: Remember that you are not alone on this journey. Reach out to the people who care about you, like friends, family, and professionals. Talking to them about your challenges helps you feel like you belong and that others understand what you are going through. Their advice, understanding, and support can comfort you when things are uncertain.

Setting Goals: Make realistic goals that help you develop resilience. These goals don't have to be big; they can be small steps that lead to a sense of accomplishment. Achieving these goals makes you feel more confident and motivated to keep going. Each success, no matter how small, shows you that you can overcome obstacles.

Learning from Resilient Role Models: Get inspiration from people who have overcome tough times. Resilient role models show you how to stay strong in the face of challenges. Their stories teach you about the strategies and attitudes that helped them thrive. Learning from their experiences gives you useful insights that guide you on your own path to resilience.

Building resilience is a journey that goes on and on. Every time you reflect, cope well, connect with others, or learn from others, you become stronger and better at facing change and tough times.

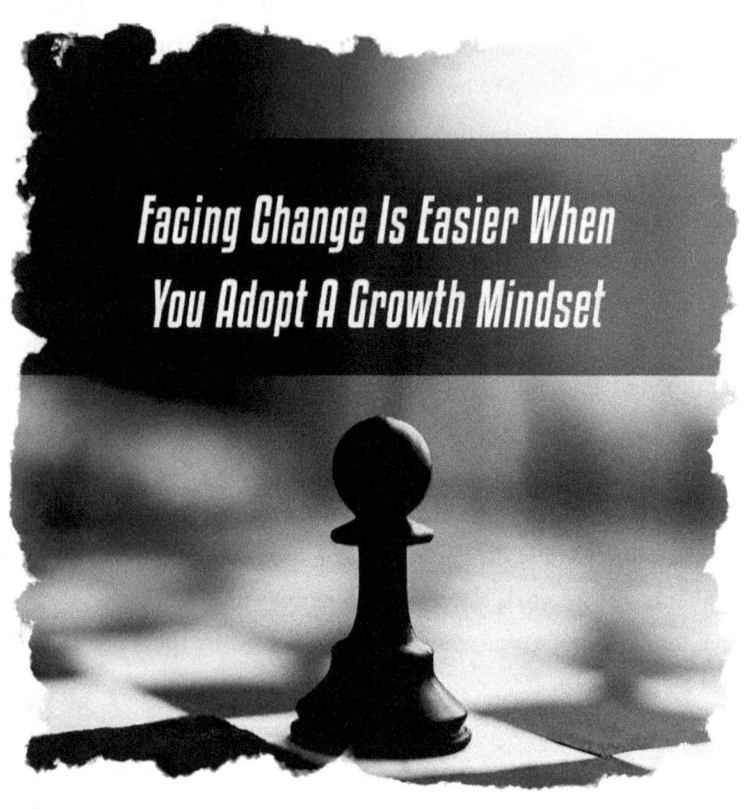

Chapter 12

Step 1 – Recognize the Change

"Courageously acknowledging change is like stepping into the light of understanding. Embrace this illumination, for within it lies the wisdom to navigate the twists and turns of life's ever-evolving path."

Realizing that things are changing might seem obvious, but sometimes people forget this important first step. When changes happen slowly or make us uncomfortable, it's easy to ignore the small shifts that are gradually changing how things are. However, if you become aware of what's happening, you can respond thoughtfully instead of just reacting without thinking. Even a small change should be noticed before you do anything else.

For example, it can be hard to notice that a close friendship is getting weaker. This happens slowly over months or years as people's lives get busier. Even though both people in the friendship are not as invested as before, they don't want to change anything because it's comfortable. So, they ignore the fact that things are changing. It might seem risky to admit that the friendship is changing, but if they don't, the distance between them will only get worse. They won't realize the problem until they start talking less and feeling distant. By admitting that things are changing, they can talk about it and maybe fix the friendship before it's too late.

Changes in careers can also happen over time, usually with growing unhappiness. As people discover new things they are passionate about and get better skills, the job they used to like doesn't make them happy anymore. But thinking about changing jobs can be scary and stop them from doing anything. It's easier to keep doing a job they hate than to admit they need something different. The fear of failing in a new job is strong.

In this case too, it's really important to honestly realize that they might need a new job, even if they are not sure what that is yet. Our work changes whether we notice it or not. It's better to realize the job isn't right for them before they feel desperate and do something drastic.

Even changes in feelings and beliefs are important to notice, even though they are personal and can be hard to admit. If you start to feel disconnected from beliefs you have held for a long time, it can be too painful to think about. It's easier to push those feelings away. But avoiding the truth just makes you feel lost and anxious, especially when the changes aren't dealt with.

No matter what the situation is, it's better to realize that things are changing early on. Our minds resist change because it can be scary. But avoiding the truth doesn't help. Any changes that happen need to be noticed before we can adapt to them. If we don't realize that things are changing, we can't make good choices.

Practical steps to Recognizing Change

Recognizing change is a crucial skill in navigating the complexities of life. Change can manifest in various forms, from minor shifts in our daily routines to major transformations in our personal and professional lives. Often, the process of recognizing change can be intricate, as it involves a blend of introspection, awareness, and openness to new possibilities. In this discussion, we will thoroughly explore the seven steps to recognizing change, offering insights into each step and how they collectively contribute to our ability to adapt and thrive in an ever-changing world.

Pause and Reflect: The modern world is bustling with activity, and it's easy to get caught up in the whirlwind of our routines. However, recognizing change requires us to take deliberate moments of pause. By stepping back and reflecting on your surroundings, experiences, and interactions, you will create an opportunity to observe any deviations from the norm. This pause serves as a mental reset that allows you to detach from the automatic patterns you often fall into. It's akin to temporarily stepping off a moving train to assess your surroundings before rejoining the journey.

Stay Open-Minded: Change is not always overt. Sometimes, it presents itself in subtle ways that require us to be receptive to new information and perspectives. An open mind is a gateway to recognizing these nuances. When you approach situations with preconceived notions, you might overlook shifts that don't align with your assumptions. Staying open-minded means being curious and willing to consider alternative viewpoints. It's like opening a window to let in fresh air – it invigorates your ability to perceive change, even when it's not immediately obvious.

Comparison to the Past: Our memories of the past serve as a benchmark for what is considered "normal" or "usual." By comparing your current situation to how things were in the past, you can identify deviations that signal change. It's like placing two puzzle pieces side by side to see if they fit together. Even the slightest misalignment can be a clue that change has occurred. This step encourages you to be mindful of the details and intricacies that might otherwise go unnoticed.

Listen to Feedback: The people around us are valuable sources of insight. They observe us from different vantage points and can detect changes that we might be too close to notice. By actively seeking and listening to feedback, you open yourself to diverse perspectives. This step requires humility – the willingness to acknowledge that others might see things you don't. Just as a conductor relies on feedback from musicians to shape an orchestra's performance, we rely on feedback from those around us to harmonize with the changes in our environment.

Question Assumptions: Assumptions are mental shortcuts we take to make sense of the world. While they can be helpful, they can also blind you to change. As you encounter new situations, it's essential to question assumptions about how things should be. This step demands intellectual courage – the willingness to challenge your own beliefs. It's like exploring uncharted territory with a curious mindset, willing to uncover hidden treasures of change that lie beneath the surface.

Monitor Trends: Change is often driven by trends and developments that shape our world. Staying informed about these trends is akin to having a radar that detects shifts on the horizon. This step involves active engagement with information – reading, researching, and staying updated about developments in our field or area of interest. Just as a ship captain monitors weather patterns to navigate rough seas, we monitor trends to navigate the currents of change.

Trust Your Intuition: Intuition is a powerful tool that taps into our subconscious observations and experiences. Sometimes, our gut feeling can be the first indicator that change is afoot. Trusting your intuition means honoring your inner voice and giving it a seat at the table of decision-making. It's like having an early warning system that alerts you to the approaching winds of change. This step encourages us to integrate both rational analysis and intuitive insights to form a comprehensive understanding of change.

In conclusion, recognizing change is a multidimensional process that draws from various aspects of our cognitive and emotional faculties. These steps provide a comprehensive framework for maximizing our ability to perceive and adapt to change. In an era defined by rapid and transformative shifts, mastering this skill is not merely advantageous – it's essential for personal growth, professional success, and overall well-being.

A Practical Guide

You see, this guide will help you apply the steps listed in any environment, aspect or field of life or your emotions. But I will use a work environment as an example so you can understand the process involved.

Imagine you are starting a new job at a company known for its innovative approach to business. As you settle into your role, you notice that things seem a bit different from what you expected. Let's walk through the seven steps of recognizing change in this scenario.

Step 1: Pause and Reflect

In this bustling workplace, where colleagues are always on the move, you decide to take a moment to pause. During your lunch break, you find a quiet corner and give yourself some time to think. You reflect on your first few days at the office, your interactions with colleagues, and the tasks you have been assigned. This pause gives you the chance to step back and see the bigger picture.

Step 2: Stay Open-Minded

As you attend team meetings and engage in conversations, you notice that your colleagues often discuss new and innovative ideas. These ideas sometimes challenge traditional ways of doing things. While you might have expected a more conventional approach, you remind yourself to stay open-minded. You realize that this company encourages fresh thinking and that change might come in unexpected forms.

Step 3: Comparison to the Past

You think back to your previous job, where meetings were more structured and formal. In contrast, your current workplace seems to have a more relaxed and collaborative atmosphere. You realize that the approach to meetings has shifted, and this comparison makes you aware of the change in communication styles.

Step 4: Listen to Feedback

During a coffee break, you strike up a conversation with a colleague who has been at the company for a while. As you chat, they mention that the company has been implementing new strategies to adapt to market trends. They also share how these changes have affected their own role. This feedback helps you understand that the company is actively responding to shifts in the industry.

Step 5: Question Assumptions

In your previous job, you were used to following a specific workflow for projects. However, you notice that your team here approaches projects in a more flexible manner. Initially, you assume that the old way must be better. But then you remind yourself to question this assumption. Why does it have to be one way or the other? This mental shift allows you to consider the benefits of both approaches.

Step 6: Monitor Trends

During your spare time, you start reading industry news and articles related to your field. You come across reports about how technology is revolutionizing the way businesses operate. You realize that these trends are relevant to your company's direction. This newfound awareness of industry trends helps you connect the dots between external changes and what's happening within your workplace.

Step 7: Trust Your Intuition

As you attend more meetings and collaborate with your team, you start to feel a sense of excitement about the new possibilities that the company's approach brings. Although you can't pinpoint exactly what's changed, your intuition tells you that there's a different energy in the air. You trust this gut feeling and embrace the positive vibe that comes with it.

In this scenario, you have successfully navigated the steps of recognizing change. By taking the time to pause, staying open-minded, comparing to the past, listening to feedback, questioning assumptions, monitoring trends, and trusting your intuition, you have gained a comprehensive understanding of the changes occurring in your new work environment.

By following these steps, you have become adept at spotting even the most subtle shifts. Whether it's adapting to new communication styles, embracing innovative ideas, or aligning with the company's evolving strategies, your ability to recognize change equips you to thrive in this dynamic work setting.

Chapter 13

Step 2 – Define The Change

"Define the winds of change that sweep through your life, for in their direction lies the compass of understanding. With clarity as your guide, you navigate uncharted waters with purpose and resilience."

Once you realize that things are changing, the next important step is to figure out what's changing and how it's happening. Change can feel unclear until we give it a clear description. This helps us focus on what's happening and gives us direction. Defining the changes helps us see the details and understand why they matter.

For example, saying "My mom's memory is getting worse" doesn't give us a clear picture. But if we ask more questions, we can figure out what's really going on. Is she having trouble remembering recent things, like our conversations? Or is she getting lost even on familiar roads? Defining the changes in detail helps us know what to do next.

Defining things also helps us understand ourselves better. Saying "I feel stressed and lazy at work" is a start. But if we say "I'm feeling burned out because my job gives me too much to do," it helps us see that it's not just us, but the situation causing the problem.

When we describe changes, it also helps the people around us understand what's happening. If we suddenly quit our job, people might not know why. But if we say "I'm leaving because my mental health is suffering from too much stress," people will understand and be supportive. Describing changes isn't just for big things; even small changes can benefit from it. Saying "I've been getting angry easily because I'm not sleeping enough" is better than thinking we're just being irrational. Saying "I'm not happy with my job because I've grown beyond it" helps us know what to do next.

Above all, taking the time to describe what's changing helps us understand it better, it might be hard at first, because our minds prefer to stay comfortable. But taking the time to define changes makes it easier to deal with them. It's like having a map to guide us through the unknown. Describing changes is a way to empower ourselves and make sense of our journey.

Here are some more tips for effectively defining changes:

Get specific: Avoid vague descriptions like "things are different now." Pinpoint precise aspects that have changed, like behaviors, attitudes, priorities, habits, etc. Details create focus.

Quantify when possible: Include measurable facts and data. Defining a change in income by its exact dollar or percentage shift makes the impact concrete. Quantification highlights the magnitude of change.

Contrast past and present: Compare the present situation to well-defined past baselines. This contrast reveals the essence of change. "I used to socialize twice a week, now it's once a month" tells the story.

Name impacts: Articulate how the change is impacting you and others. "This career change means less income but more time with family." Defining downstream effects exposes ripple results.

Explain context: Provide context around why changes may be occurring, like life stage evolutions, new environments, or catalyst events. This frames the meaning rather than leaving changes mysterious.

Track path: Note whether changes seem to progress linearly, accelerate, or plateau. Defining momentum guides appropriate responses.

Weigh positives and negatives: Identify beneficial aspects of a change alongside challenges. A balanced view reduces likelihood of overreactions fueled solely by difficulty.

Revise definitions over time: Initial definitions will expand as changes unfold. Revisit and update definitions regularly to incorporate new observations.

The goal is a definition concise yet nuanced. With care and courage, we can transition changes from disorienting ambiguity into clearly delineated maps that guide our path to positive growth.

Application Guidelines

Take for instance, a young woman named Maya who has recently graduated from college and is entering a new phase of her life. As she embarks on this journey, she encounters changes that she needs to define and understand. Let's explore how Maya applies the step-by-step guide to effectively define these changes in her life.

Step 1: Get Specific:

Maya notices that things are different now that she's out of college. Instead of just saying "life has changed," she gets specific. She realizes that her behaviors have changed; she's now waking up earlier, spending more time job hunting, and going to bed later. These precise details help her focus on what exactly has changed.

Step 2: Quantify When Possible:

Maya decides to quantify some of the changes. For example, she used to spend about 3 hours a day on social media, but now it's down to 1 hour. She also notes that her savings account had $1000, and after her new job, it has increased to $1500. These numbers provide concrete evidence of the changes happening in her life.

Step 3: Contrast Past and Present:

Maya contrasts her past college routine with her current situation. She realizes that in college, she used to have classes every day, hang out with friends almost every evening, and have a more relaxed schedule. Now, her days are filled with job applications, interviews, and adapting to a new work routine. This comparison helps her define the key differences in her daily life.

Step 4: Name Impacts:

Maya thinks about how these changes are impacting her. She acknowledges that her new job is bringing in a steady income, which is a positive impact. On the other hand, she misses spending as much time with her friends and feels a bit more stressed due to the responsibilities of her job search. Naming these impacts helps her understand the balance between the positives and challenges.

Step 5: Explain Context:

Maya considers the context around her changes. She realizes that graduating from college is a major life transition, and it makes sense that her routines would shift. She also acknowledges that job hunting and starting a career are natural progressions after completing her education. This context helps her see that change is a normal part of life's journey.

Step 6: Track Trajectory:

Maya notices that some changes are happening gradually, while others seem to be accelerating. For instance, her confidence in interviews has been increasing steadily as she gains more experience.

On the other hand, she feels that her free time is decreasing faster than she anticipated due to her busy schedule. This tracking of changes' trajectories helps her predict what might happen next.

Step 7: Weigh Positives and Negatives:

Maya takes a moment to list the positives and negatives of her current situation. On the positive side, she's learning new skills at her job, and her financial situation is improving. However, she misses spending time with her friends and feels the pressure of job interviews. Weighing these aspects helps her maintain a balanced perspective on the changes she's experiencing.

Step 8: Revise Definitions over Time:

Maya knows that her definitions of these changes might evolve as she continues her journey. She plans to revisit her initial definitions regularly and update them based on new observations and experiences. She understands that change is dynamic, and her understanding of it will also grow over time.

Through these steps, Maya is effectively defining the changes she's encountering as she transitions from college to her career. By being specific, quantifying changes, contrasting past and present, naming impacts, explaining context, tracking trajectories, weighing positives and negatives, and planning to revise her definitions, she's creating a clear map to navigate the changes in her life. This approach helps her embrace change with confidence and navigate her path to positive growth.

Chapter 14

Step 3 – Don't Let the Change Define You

"Change is the river of life, and your identity is the riverbank. Let its waters flow around you, shaping you without ever diminishing your essence."

After recognizing and defining a change, the next vital mindset shift is refusing to let the change define you. By separating your identity from difficult changes occurring, you avoid compounding challenges with crises of self-concept and self-image. Too often, you might interpret transitions like job loss, illnesses, or relationship breakdowns as sentences on your personal self-worth. "I'm a failure because I got fired." "This diagnosis means I'm defective." "My ex leaving reveals I'm unlovable." You let a single change obscure every other facet of life and self.

In reality, changes speak to temporary situations, not innate identity. Losing a job reflects corporate priorities, not lack of talent. Disease results from cellular processes, not personal flaws. A breakup stems from two individuals growing apart, not one's inadequacy alone. Yet when change shakes your world, your mind fixates on self-blame interpretations. Why? Because subconsciously you prefer to believe you can control outcomes. If you caused the change, then avoiding the "mistake" again restores stability. But change always involves complex forces far beyond just individual will.

The mind also equates loss of things and roles with loss of self. But your essence exists far above external signifiers that inevitably shift through life phases. You are more than any job title, relationship status, age, location, or health condition. These represent but brief seasons, not ultimate value.

Of course, radical changes rightfully impact your self-concept. But total redefinition based on one change sets you up for shame and paralysis. Let the change expand your identity, not overwhelm it. See both continuity and discontinuity between your past, present, and future self. Growth emerges from evolution, not erasure.

Ask what positive traits you draw on to navigate this challenge that remain untouched by surface-level shifts? How do you want this change to reshape you into someone stronger, wiser, and more compassionate? Use mirrors of loved ones to reflect back your enduring essence beneath day-to-day turbulence.

With perspective, you prevent temporary changes from casting permanent shadows over your entire being. Your self-concept becomes like a majestic mountain, weathering storms and seasons yet never wholly defined by them. Defeat fixed mindsets that equate an experience with destiny or self-worth. The healthiest self-images integrate change as part of a greater unfolding journey.

Ensuring a change does not define you, especially a negative change.

Separate Situation from Self: Remember that the change says nothing about your worth or identity. Getting laid off reflects company priorities, not your competence. Illness results from cellular processes, not defects in character. A breakup happens because two people grew apart, not because you are unlovable. The situation is not you.

Expand Your Lens: Don't let one change eclipse your whole reality. You are more than any job title, relationship status, home, role, or condition. These are roles you play and experiences you have, not your essence. Keep perspective on all unchanged parts of your life and self.

Focus on Continuity: Consider what positive traits sustain you through this change. How do you want to grow from it? Reflect on who you were before, during, and after the change. There is continuity between these versions of you. Let go of false assumptions about transformation requiring erasing the past you.

Don't Personalize: Remember that external factors cause most changes, not individual mistakes. Job loss reflects company priorities, diseases have biological causes, relationships end from complex reasons. Do not blame solely yourself or see it as punishment. It's an experience, not a verdict on you.

Reframe Positively: Ask how this change allows you to shed limiting past definitions of yourself to uncover new potential and purpose. Use it as a catalyst for embracing dormant parts of who you are. Be defined by your inspiring response, not the change itself.

Cherish Relationships: Lean on loved ones who appreciate your enduring good essence despite the current challenge. Their care reflects back your wholeness and gives courage to persevere. You are still you.

Practice Self-Compassion: Treat yourself kindly, as you would a good friend in this situation. Counter harmful self-criticism that breeds shame. Understand this change says nothing about your value. Show yourself the grace and love you deserve.

As you ground yourself in truth, you avoid letting changes shake your foundations. Your self-concept becomes like a majestic mountain, transformed but never defined by passing seasons and storms. You are far more than what happens to you.

Negative consequences of allowing a change define you

Damaged self-image: If you believe a failure or setback exposes your inadequacy, your overall self-confidence and identity suffers. Seeing yourself only through that lens distorts your bigger picture.

Learned helplessness: Thinking you caused a change through personal defect fosters helpless resignation rather than empowerment to act. "I'm unlovable" paralyzes more than "The relationship ended because we grew apart."

Shame and withdrawal: Internalizing failure often breeds overwhelming shame. This causes withdrawing from others who could provide support and perspective. Isolation makes the shame more severe.

Loss of hope: Letting a change define you can lead to losing hope anything will improve. If the change seems due to fixed personal flaws, the future looks static rather than open to growth.

Shortsighted decisions: In intense emotion, we may make dramatic decisions assuming the worst of ourselves, like impulsively quitting a job. These often prove unwise in hindsight.

Loss of resilience: Defining self-worth by external situations weakens ability to bounce back from adversities. Small failures more easily spiral without separating self from circumstance.

Stunted growth: Over-identifying with a negative change freezes us in place rather than learning from it. No evolution results from catastrophizing a setback rather than reframing it.

Above all, avoiding excessive self-blame for changes prevents amplifying their pain immensely. With perspective, you gain resilience to integrate experiences into growth, not paralysis.

Chapter 15

Step 4 – Weigh The Pros And Cons Of Taking Action

"Thoughtful contemplation is the compass that guides wise adaptation in the face of change."

After recognizing, defining, and separating self from a change, thoughtful contemplation and assessment set wise adaptation in motion. A balanced accounting of potential benefits and drawbacks provides crucial perspective. This step is important because as a human when life changes arise, your first instinct may be to immediately act to address them. But jumping into action without thoughtful weighing the pros and cons often backfires. You end up running into situations and making decisions you will later regret. That is why pausing to fully map out potential benefits and drawbacks is so essential before altering course.

Creating space to reflect protects you from knee-jerk reactions rooted in emotion rather than reason. It guards against overvaluing short-term comforts that jeopardize long-term fulfillment. Weighing change helps ground you in core values rather than reacting to surface fears or desires.

Taking time to brainstorm all imaginable pros gives you the chance to envision positive outcomes obscured by initial discomfort. You envision how pivoting could increase happiness, free up time for passions, reduce stress, improve health, and unlock exciting new directions. A world of possibility reveals itself once denial lifts.

Likewise, diligently listing cons makes conscious the risks and trade-offs change represents. You realistically assess downsides like time investment required, effects on relationships, financial insecurity, loss of stability, the unknowns ahead. Averting blindness to costs allows managing them.

By writing out both sides in tangible form, you gain balanced perspective. Looking at change through the lens of impact rather than emotion defuses anxiety's distortion. You make space for soul searching about what matters most to your life vision.

Approaching change with intentionality rather than impulse provides a firm foundation. When you have carefully weighed the landscape ahead, you can take confident steps forward. Your eyes are wide open, not squinting to avoid truth.

With seasoned understanding, you become nimble to pivot as circumstances evolve. Weighing change is not a one-time event, but a habitual practice to frame transitions with wisdom. This equips you to handle whatever life brings with poise, conviction and grace. The only path is ahead.

Step by step practical Guideline for weighing pros and cons of taking action.

Creating Two Columns: Start by drawing a line down a sheet of paper dividing it in two columns. Title one column "Pros" and the other "Cons." This layout helps you map out the positive and negative aspects of the change visually. Seeing both sides in writing stimulates balanced contemplation.

Brainstorming Possibilities: In the Pros column, brainstorm every possible advantage, benefit, upside, or opportunity you can think of for moving forward with the change. List increased happiness, better health, exciting options, potential for growth, income gains, more free time, etc. Capture every pro that comes to mind.

Then thoroughly list potential negatives like risks, disadvantages, downsides, or costs of making the change in the Cons column. Include loss of stability, income dips, disagreement from others, sunk costs abandoning the current situation, decreased free time, unknowns, etc.

Reviewing and Refining: Read over the full lists and refine them by grouping similar ideas together and highlighting the most weighty factors. Put stars next to the items you feel carry the most significance based on your core values and life vision. Eliminate repetitive or trivial points.

Adding Supporting Details: For the starred key factors, add a sentence explaining why each one matters so much and how it would impact your life positively or negatively. Sharing the backstory brings salience to why something makes your Pro or Con list, and elevates its importance above superficial points.

Assigning Relative Weight: On a 1-5 scale, rate the significance of every item with 1 being relatively inconsequential and 5 being extremely important and impactful to your life. This numerical rating based on your personal priorities illuminates which pros and cons deserve greatest consideration for you specifically. It reveals which truly tip the scales.

Noting Timeframes: Additionally, label each factor short-term or long-term. Tracking timeframes helps balance instant gratification against lasting fulfillment. Often short term ease leads to long term costs, while short term sacrifices enable long term happiness. Discerning this helps wise decision making.

Identifying Mitigations: For serious cons concerning you, carefully consider any actions that could reduce their likelihood or severity if you proceed with change. Outlining concrete mitigating steps like added planning, training, outside support etc., makes some cons feel less formidable.

Checking Emotions: Step back and review the full balanced pro/con lists from a calm, rational mindset. Make sure fears or anxiety about uncertainty are not disproportionately overinflating the downsides and cons. Rely on reason more than emotions clouded by past biases.

Sitting with the Insights: The last stage is to reflect on the insights gained by this thorough weighing of potential changes before finalizing next actions. Moving slowly with care now prevents hasty reactions soon regretted. Patience yields perspective; wisdom conquers confusion.

Chapter 16

Step 5 – Make The Proper Preparations

"Preparation is the ignition that sparks success, equipping us with the tools to light up our path with clarity and confidence."

The Five Powers of Preparation

Preparation is the key to success. It equips us with the tools, knowledge, and confidence to tackle challenges head-on and make the most of opportunities. Let's explore the five powers that effective preparation brings to our lives.

Clarity and Confidence: Preparation provides us with a clear roadmap. When we prepare, we gather information, plan strategies, and set achievable goals. This clarity boosts our confidence because we know what to expect and how to handle it. Think of it like studying for an exam – when you have covered the material, you are more confident in your ability to answer questions accurately.

Adaptability and Resilience: Preparation arms us with a flexible mindset. By anticipating different scenarios, we're better equipped to handle unexpected twists. It's like packing an umbrella for a trip, even if the forecast is sunny – you are ready for changes. With preparation, setbacks become stepping stones, and challenges become opportunities to learn and grow.

Efficiency and Effectiveness: When we prepare, we streamline our actions. Having a plan in place saves time and energy. Just like a chef who preps ingredients before cooking, preparation ensures a smooth process. With clear steps and organized resources, we accomplish tasks more efficiently, leaving room for other pursuits and reducing stress.

Magnetism of Opportunities: Preparation attracts opportunities. When we're ready, we recognize chances that others might miss. It's like having a fishing net ready when the fish start to bite. By cultivating knowledge, skills, and a proactive attitude, we become magnets for prospects, advancement, and growth.

Empowerment and Control: Preparation empowers us to shape our destiny. We're in control when we're prepared – we steer our course instead of being swept by the currents. Like a captain navigating a ship, we set the direction. By preparing, we're not at the mercy of circumstances; we're masters of our own journey.

Preparing to Take Action in Response to a Change

The preparation we are talking about here is the process by which you lay the groundwork for action in regards to change. According to the previous steps we have discussed in line with dealing with change, there may be no action to take at all, but if there is need for an action then you need to properly prepare.

This step is very important, it means you are committing to act on the change that happened. This is where you begin to take control of what might have been an entirely uncontrollable situation. Maybe the change was that you got demoted at work. Your knee-jerk reaction is to be upset. You can't believe they did this. You begin to rationalize in your mind how unjustly you have been treated.

After you have calmed down, you go through these seven steps to make the best out of the tough situation. You recognize the demotion. You don't judge it or take sides. You define it. What happened? You got demoted. You don't say that you got demoted unfairly or justly. You simply define the change as your demotion at work. Then you weighed the pros and cons of taking action. You realized that your attendance record wasn't that great. You often called in sick or told your boss you were running late. You never stayed late when you were asked to. And honestly, you could have been a better employee.

You found out that the best course of action would be to improve your job performance in many ways. You could also take classes your employer offers to make yourself more valuable. You realize your demotion was heavily influenced by your performance.

Chapter 17

Step 6 – Take Action

"Action is the catalyst that turns the wheels of change. Embrace the power of doing to bring your vision to life and create a brighter future."

Making Change Happen

After getting ready and making necessary preparations, it's time to do something. You need to change the things you do that lead to bad results. Just thinking won't help; you have to act. Sitting and waiting won't solve problems. If the change was something you couldn't control, what can you do to be ready next time? This is what you figured out in the last step. Taking action means making changes in what you do to get better results.

Taking action is like driving a car after planning the route. You can't just sit in the car; you have to start the engine and drive. It's about doing things differently to make good changes happen. The desire for positive results should push you to act. You are not just thinking anymore; you are doing something about it. This desire gives you energy and keeps you going, even when things are tough.

Taking action means moving from thinking to doing. It's like going from watching a game to playing in it. You become an active part of the change process. Not doing anything is a mistake. You can't sit and wait for good things to happen because change needs effort to make it work.

It's not just about now; it's about the future too. What you do now affects what happens later. Taking action prepares you for future challenges and helps you grow.

Taking action doesn't only apply to current change; it sets you up for more changes in the future. It's like training for a game – you build skills that help you perform better every time. By taking action, you take charge of the change. It's you saying, "I'm responsible for making this change work." You are in control, and that's a powerful feeling.

Even if the change isn't in your control, you can still act. You can learn new things, build resilience, and connect with others. These actions make you better prepared for whatever comes next.

It's about making change real, not just a dream. By taking action, you move forward, create results, and show that you are ready for whatever comes your way.

The Place of Discipline While taking Action

When you make the decision to embrace change and take action towards it, you are embarking on a transformative journey. However, this journey is rarely a smooth one. It is filled with challenges, uncertainties, and moments that test your determination. This is where discipline steps in, playing a pivotal role in keeping you on track even when things get tough.

Change is a dynamic process, and your initial enthusiasm might give way to discomfort as you navigate unfamiliar territory. The road of taking action towards embracing change or changing the change often brings unexpected obstacles that can shake your confidence. People whom you counted on for support might back away, and the path you envisioned might prove more difficult than you anticipated. These are the moments when your commitment to embracing change and taking action is put to the test.

In the face of such challenges, discipline emerges as a guiding force, discipline is the determined commitment to stay on the course of your intended action irrespective of the obstacles that arise. It is the determination to push forward even when the journey becomes difficult. Discipline acts as a counterforce against feelings of doubt and discouragement, reminding you of the bigger picture and the positive outcomes that await on the other side of hardship. It transforms your intentions into tangible actions and ensure you do not back out no matter the challenges. It's the bridge that connects your desire for change and action with the effort required to make it happen. It propels you to move beyond mere contemplation and translate your aspirations into concrete steps. It signifies a shift from passive intentions to active engagement, reinforcing your commitment to achieving meaningful transformation.

In the face of setbacks and unexpected challenges while taking action, discipline becomes the compass that guides you through the storm. Rather than being derailed by adversity, discipline empowers you to view obstacles as opportunities for growth. It instills in you the belief that difficulties are not roadblocks but stepping stones on your path to success. Through discipline, setbacks become stepping stones to further strengthen your resolve and determination.

The role of discipline extends beyond persevering through challenges; it encompasses self-care and resilience-building. Discipline is the understanding that your journey is not solely about enduring discomfort but also about making wise decisions for your well-being. It emphasizes the importance of taking breaks when necessary, replenishing your energy, and maintaining your physical and emotional health.

At its core, discipline draws from your inner strength and conviction. It's the inner voice that reminds you of your goals, urging you to continue despite the difficulties. Discipline empowers you to choose a path of progress over stagnation, even when external circumstances are unfavorable. It's the conscious decision to prioritize your long-term goals over the allure of immediate comfort. It is not just about the present; it's an investment in your future self. By nurturing discipline, you cultivate a mindset of resilience and determination that will serve you well in times to come. It equips you with the tools to navigate future challenges with grace and strength, ensuring that you are better prepared to face adversity.

Above all, discipline is the cornerstone that ensures you stay with your intended action and you do not chicken out when things get uneasy, discipline transforms your desire into a reality. It differentiates between those who make momentary efforts and those who achieve lasting transformation. Through discipline, you gain the strength to stay true to your intentions, even when circumstances become challenging. It's the unwavering force that keeps you focused on your journey, enabling you to emerge victorious despite the obstacles.

Cultivating Discipline – Practical Steps to Build Strength and Consistency

Discipline is the cornerstone of achieving goals, navigating challenges, and realizing lasting change. It's the internal compass that guides us toward intentional actions, even when faced with difficulties. Developing discipline is not only essential but also attainable with the right strategies and mindset. Follow this practical steps to help you build discipline in various aspects of your life.

Set Clear Goals: Having clear and specific goals provides a sense of direction. Define what you want to achieve and break it down into manageable steps. Clear goals serve as a roadmap, making it easier to stay disciplined as you work towards them.

Create a Routine: Establishing a daily routine helps build consistency. Design a schedule that includes dedicated time for the actions aligned with your goals. A routine eliminates the need for constant decision-making, making it easier to stick to your desired actions.

Prioritize Tasks: Identify tasks that contribute most to your goals and prioritize them. Focus on tasks that align with your values and bring you closer to your desired outcomes. Prioritization prevents distractions from derailing your progress.

Practice Self-Control: Self-control is a cornerstone of discipline. Train yourself to resist immediate gratification in favor of long-term benefits. This might involve delaying rewards, resisting temptations, and making choices that align with your goals.

Break Tasks into Small Steps: Large tasks can feel overwhelming, leading to procrastination. Break them into smaller, manageable steps. Achieving these smaller milestones gives you a sense of accomplishment and fuels your motivation to continue.

Maintain Consistency: Consistency is key to building discipline. Commit to your chosen actions regularly, even when motivation wanes. Consistency turns actions into habits, making them easier to maintain over time.

Hold Yourself Accountable: Accountability is a powerful motivator. Share your goals with a friend, mentor, or coach who can provide support and hold you responsible for your actions. Knowing that someone is tracking your progress can boost your commitment.

Practice Time Management: Effective time management ensures that you allocate sufficient time to tasks that matter. Set specific time blocks for your desired actions and stick to them. Avoid multitasking, as it can dilute your focus.

Visual Reminders: Use visual cues to remind yourself of your goals. Post motivational quotes, images, or your goals in visible places. These reminders keep your objectives at the forefront of your mind.

Embrace the 2-Minute Rule: If a task can be completed in two minutes or less, do it immediately. This prevents small tasks from accumulating and overwhelming you later. Completing quick tasks also boosts your sense of accomplishment.

Practice Mindfulness: Mindfulness helps you stay present and focused. Engage in practices like meditation, deep breathing, or journaling to enhance your awareness and self-discipline.

Reward Yourself: Celebrate your achievements, even the small ones. Rewarding yourself acknowledges your progress and reinforces positive behavior. Choose rewards that align with your goals and avoid those that contradict your efforts.

Learn from Setbacks: Setbacks are a natural part of any journey. Instead of letting them derail your discipline, view them as opportunities to learn and grow. Analyze what went wrong, adjust your approach, and move forward with renewed determination.

Surround Yourself with Positivity: Surround yourself with people who support your goals and encourage your efforts. Positive influences can provide motivation and make it easier to stay disciplined.

Focus on the Process, Not Just the Outcome: While outcomes are important, focus on the process itself. Enjoy the journey of growth and self-improvement. This perspective reduces the pressure and allows you to stay committed regardless of the immediate results.

Practice Self-Care: Self-care is essential for maintaining discipline. Ensure you're getting enough rest, eating healthily, and engaging in activities that rejuvenate you. A well-cared-for body and mind are better equipped to stay disciplined.

Stay Resilient: Discipline requires resilience. Understand that setbacks and challenges are part of the journey. Embrace failures as learning experiences and bounce back with renewed determination.

Seek Continuous Improvement: Discipline isn't about perfection; it's about consistent improvement. Continuously evaluate your progress, identify areas for growth, and make adjustments to your strategies.

Embrace Flexibility: While discipline involves sticking to a plan, it also requires flexibility. Be open to adjusting your approach as circumstances change. Adaptation is a sign of strength, not weakness.

Cultivating discipline is an ongoing drive that requires effort, commitment, and intention, it will not happen in a day. By implementing these practical steps, you can develop the strength to stay consistent, focused, and resilient in the face of challenges. Discipline is not about being rigid but about channeling your energy towards meaningful actions that are in line with your goals. As you nurture discipline, you empower yourself to make lasting changes, achieve your aspirations, and live a more fulfilling and purposeful life.

Chapter 18

Step 7 – Practice Proper Maintenance

"Just as a garden thrives with consistent care, so does change flourish with ongoing maintenance. Nurture your transformation to see it grow and bear fruit."

Sustaining Change through Ongoing Maintenance

I need you to understand that this is a vital step towards lasting transformation. As you embark on the journey of giving change a chance, each step brings you closer to embracing transformation and experiencing growth. Amidst the excitement and challenges, there's a crucial phase that often goes overlooked – the step of practicing proper maintenance. This step is like nurturing a newly planted seed to ensure it grows into a flourishing tree.

Maintenance, in the context of change, involves regular and intentional efforts to ensure the sustainability of the chosen course of action. It is a commitment to consistently evaluate, adjust, and optimize your approach to the change you have initiated. Just as you wouldn't build a house without a strong foundation, you cannot expect change to endure without proper maintenance.

Change, whether big or small, requires ongoing attention to thrive. Without maintenance, even the most well-intentioned actions can lose their impact over time. Maintenance serves as a safeguard against slipping back into old habits, ensuring that the positive effects of change become ingrained in your lifestyle.

Proper maintenance starts with regular review, this involves periodically evaluating your progress since initiating the change. Take a step back and objectively analyze whether the actions you have taken are yielding the desired results. Assess whether the change has brought the anticipated benefits and consider any areas that need improvement.

Reflection is an integral part of maintenance, it's a time for introspection and candid self-assessment. Ask yourself whether the change aligns with your goals and values. Reflect on whether your actions are consistent with the intended outcome. If adjustments are needed, embrace them without hesitation. Flexibility is essential, as it allows you to adapt your approach based on your evolving understanding.

Another thing is that mistakes are inevitable, even in the pursuit of positive change, maintenance provides the opportunity to learn from these mistakes. Instead of viewing missteps as failures, consider them as valuable lessons. Reflect on what went wrong, why it happened, and how you can avoid similar pitfalls in the future. Learning from mistakes is an integral part of growth.

Proper maintenance is instrumental in reinforcing positive habits because you consistently practice new behaviors, they gradually become ingrained in your routine. Maintenance helps prevent the regression to old patterns and ensures that the positive changes you have initiated become second nature.

Every journey is unique, and change is no exception. Maintenance empowers you to adjust your strategies based on your unique circumstances. What worked for someone else might not yield the same results for you. Regularly evaluating your progress allows you to fine-tune your approach to best suit your needs and goals.

Overcoming Setbacks

Challenges and setbacks are part of any change process and maintenance equips you with the resilience to overcome these hurdles. It's a time to reassess your commitment and determination. By addressing challenges head-on, you reinforce your resolve to stay the course and keep moving forward. Change is not static; it evolves as you progress. Maintenance ensures that your chosen actions remain aligned with your evolving goals. It's about making necessary adjustments to accommodate shifts in your aspirations, circumstances, or external factors.

So, I tell you practicing proper maintenance is the linchpin that secures the sustainability of change. It solidifies the gains you have made, prevents regression to old habits, and empowers you to evolve with your goals. Embracing maintenance means embracing growth as an ongoing journey rather than a fleeting destination. As you embark on the path of practicing proper maintenance, remember that you're nurturing the seeds of change you have sown, ensuring they blossom into a beautiful garden of transformation and fulfillment.

A Review of the Seven Steps to Accepting Change

Change is an inevitable force in life, constantly pushing us to adapt, evolve, and grow. However, despite its inevitability, many of us struggle to embrace change wholeheartedly. We often find ourselves resisting it, fearing the unknown, and clinging to the familiar. It's in these moments that a well-structured approach can serve as a guiding light, helping us not only embrace change but also manage it effectively. The seven-step approach to change offers a comprehensive framework that empowers individuals to navigate change with confidence, clarity, and resilience.

Step 1 – Recognize the Change: The Starting Point

Recognition is the cornerstone of any meaningful change journey. This first step is where you acknowledge the presence of change and its impact on your life. It's about facing reality head-on and dispelling any denial that may prevent you from moving forward. Recognizing change requires self-awareness, introspection, and a willingness to confront discomfort. This step paves the way for honest self-assessment, enabling you to accurately perceive the scope and nature of the change.

Step 2 – Define the Change: Clarity in Chaos

Once you have recognized the change, it's imperative to define it clearly. This step involves gaining a deep understanding of what the change entails, its implications, and how it affects you and your surroundings. Defining the change provides clarity in the midst of chaos, enabling you to dispel ambiguity and misconceptions. It involves asking critical questions: What is the nature of this change? How does it impact me? What are the expected outcomes? By answering these questions, you empower yourself to approach the change with a sense of purpose and direction.

Step 3 – Don't Let the Change Define You: Taking Ownership

In the face of change, it's common to allow it to define our identity and dictate our reactions. However, the third step emphasizes the importance of maintaining your sense of self amidst change. Your identity is not solely defined by external circumstances; it's shaped by your values, beliefs, and aspirations. Taking ownership of your identity empowers you to respond to change in alignment with your core principles. It's about understanding that while change may influence your circumstances, it need not alter the essence of who you are.

Step 4 – Weigh the Pros and Cons of Taking Action: Informed Decision-Making

The fourth step introduces the concept of deliberate decision-making. Change often presents us with choices – whether to take action or remain passive. Weighing the pros and cons of these choices enables you to make informed decisions. Delving into the potential benefits and drawbacks of various actions equips you with a comprehensive perspective. It encourages you to look beyond immediate outcomes and consider the long-term impact of your choices.

Step 5 – Make the Proper Preparations: Setting the Stage for Success

Preparation is a vital component of effective change management. This step involves making necessary arrangements to ensure that you're equipped to face the change successfully. It could mean acquiring new skills, gathering resources, seeking support, or cultivating a mindset of readiness. Proper preparations diminish feelings of uncertainty and vulnerability, allowing you to approach the change from a position of strength.

Step 6 – Take Action: The Catalyst for Transformation

While steps one through five lay the groundwork, step six is the catalyst for transformation. It's the bridge between contemplation and implementation. Taking action involves putting your decisions into practice and actively engaging with the change process. This step requires courage, determination, and a willingness to step out of your comfort zone. Taking action propels you forward, turning intentions into tangible results.

Step 7 – Practice Proper Maintenance: Nurturing Lasting Change

The journey of change doesn't end once action is taken; it requires ongoing care and attention. The seventh step, practicing proper maintenance, is about nurturing the changes you have initiated. It involves regularly evaluating your progress, making necessary adjustments, and ensuring that the change becomes a permanent part of your life. Maintenance prevents regression and solidifies your commitment to long-term growth.

How the Seven Steps Transform Change

Individually, each step in the seven-step approach holds its significance. Collectively, they form a comprehensive framework that empowers you to embrace change and manage it effectively. Recognizing and defining the change provide a solid foundation of understanding. Not letting the change define you and weighing the pros and cons equip you with decision-making tools. Making proper preparations and taking action bring change to life. Finally, practicing proper maintenance ensures that change endures and thrives.

Applying these steps cultivates a holistic approach to change. It empowers you to navigate change with intention, agency, and resilience. By embracing each step, you transform change from a daunting challenge into an opportunity for growth. This approach encourages you to confront change with a proactive mindset, empowering you to shape your destiny rather than being controlled by circumstances. Ultimately, the seven-step approach propels you on a journey of self-discovery, empowerment, and transformation, where change becomes a powerful ally rather than an adversary.

Conclusion

Ignoring a negative change in your life can worsen an unfortunate situation. You absolutely must face what you go through every day to have any control over the outcome. Even when there is no control over what happens, being honest about the result is the only way to get past it and move towards a healthier and more positive outlook.

Changes, big and small, are definitely going to happen. Since the human condition means change is inevitable and not always good, doesn't it make sense to recognize it? You define exactly what change really happened. This is important because sometimes we have a knee-jerk reaction to negative situations that aren't always the best response.

You learned that running from change never allows you to be as strong as you can possibly be. While much change in life is negative, you grow in so many ways when you face it head-on and overcome its negative impact.

Remembering that can make you embrace change, even when it isn't so positive. You plug in the seven-step change management system that you were just given. It's not guaranteed to keep you from experiencing negative emotions. Letting your emotions run their course is part of the healing process.

What the system above does give you is the best way to accept change. It helps you turn an unfortunate situation into the best possible reality.

To your best ever life!

Final Words

My dear reader, I need you to know that as you close the final pages of "Giving Change a Chance," you are to remember that no matter how discouraging a change might seem, there is always hope as long as there is life. Change is not the end; it's a new beginning, a chance for growth and transformation. I have come to realize that life is an adventure filled with twists and turns, and sometimes the road ahead are uncertain, dangerous and treacherous. But remember, you have within you the strength to overcome, the power to adapt, and the resilience to thrive. Challenges and changes only test your limits, but they can never extinguish the flame of hope that burns within you. Circumstances and situations will try to cast a shadow on your path, tempting you to give up. But don't let them. Hold on to hope, for it's the beacon that guides you through the darkest nights. Even when the storm is raging, there is a calm within you, a strength that refuses to be broken.

I encourage you to embrace life with open arms because each moment is an opportunity to shape your destiny. I implore you to embrace the unknown, for it holds the promise of new adventures and discoveries. Embrace change, for it's the catalyst that propels you towards your true potential.

So, as you step forward from these pages, carry with you the wisdom that change is not your enemy; No matter how formidable the challenges, no matter how overwhelming the changes, I need you to remember that hope is your constant companion. You are the author of your journey, and your story is one of resilience, courage, and triumph.

I pray that your days will be filled with hope, your heart with strength, and your spirit with unwavering determination. Embrace change, embrace life, and never give up, for within you lies the power to conquer the storms and emerge stronger on the other side.

Farewell, dear reader, and may your journey be illuminated by the eternal light of hope and happiness.

About the Book

Giving Change A Chance is an insightful and motivating guide that takes you on a journey through the process of embracing and navigating life's changes. Through practical steps, relatable examples, and inspirational quotes, this book offers a comprehensive roadmap for effectively dealing with various transitions in life.

From recognizing the need for change to taking purposeful actions and maintaining positive transformation, "Giving Change A Chance" provides a holistic approach to managing change. The book goes deep into the emotional and psychological aspects of change, emphasizing resilience, adaptability, and self-awareness.

With its practical advice and motivational content, "Giving Change A Chance" will equip you with valuable tools to confidently navigate transitions. Whether facing personal, professional, or emotional changes, this book serves as a valuable companion, offering guidance, encouragement, and practical strategies to embrace change and thrive in the face of uncertainty.

Abby's website
https://abbyadeyemi.com

PM Store Author's QR Code
https://pagemasterpublishing.ca/by/Abolade-Adeyemi/

To order more copies of this book, find books by other Canadian authors, or make inquiries about publishing your own book, contact PageMaster at:

PageMaster Publication Services Inc.
11340-120 Street, Edmonton, AB T5G 0W5
books@pagemaster.ca
780-425-9303

catalogue and e-commerce store
PageMasterPublishing.ca/Shop

About the Author

Abolade Atinuke Adeyemi, also known as Abby (née Ajiboso), is a distinguished healthcare professional whose career has been shaped by compassion, dedication, and a relentless pursuit of excellence. With nearly two decades of experience in the healthcare sector, Abby has established herself as an exceptional Manager, Healthcare Consultant, and Medical Writer.

Her journey is one of resilience, leadership, and holistic support. Beginning her career as a Registered Nurse and Registered Pediatric Nurse in Nigeria, she has since evolved into a multifaceted professional. She currently serves as a Manager, Healthcare Consultant, Medical Writer, and the CEO of Canadian Holistic Companion Inc. Her expertise spans healthcare consulting, project management, mentoring, counseling, research, and international healthcare strategies.

Abby's strong educational background includes a Ph.D. in Public Health and Geriatrics alongside an M.D. in Medicine, supplemented by an extensive list of certifications and degrees. Beyond her professional achievements, she is a devoted wife and mother of four, balancing her career with an unwavering commitment to her family.

Her dedication to positive transformation is evident through her leadership in healthcare and community services. As a founding director of RADCA (Rebuild Anti-Drug Community Agency), she actively champions community upliftment and social change.

A proud member of the Canadian Public Health Association and an accomplished author, Abby's book, Giving Change a Chance, serves as a beacon of inspiration for those seeking personal and professional transformation. Her words reflect her deep belief in the power of change and her unwavering commitment to making a meaningful impact in the world.

www.ingramcontent.com/pod-product-compliance
Lightning Source LLC
LaVergne TN
LVHW051125080426
835510LV00018B/2243